TIME PEACE

Also by Ellen Vaughn

Radical Gratitude

Kingdoms in Conflict
(Charles W. Colson and Ellen Vaughn)

Being the Body
(Charles W. Colson and Ellen Vaughn)

The God Who Hung on the Cross
(Dois Rosser and Ellen Vaughn)

Rags, Riches, and Real Success
(Dallen Peterson with Ellen Vaughn)

The Strand

Gideon's Torch
(Charles W. Colson and Ellen Vaughn)

The Body
(Charles W. Colson and Ellen Vaughn)

Against the Night
(Charles W. Colson and Ellen Vaughn)

It's All About Him
(Denise Jackson and Ellen Vaughn)

Ellen Vaughn

Living Here and Now with a Timeless God

TIME PEACE

ZONDERVAN®

ZONDERVAN.com/
AUTHORTRACKER
follow your favorite authors

 **ZONDERVAN®**

Time Peace
Copyright © 2007 by Ellen Santilli Vaughn

Requests for information should be addressed to:

Zondervan, *Grand Rapids, Michigan* 49530

Library of Congress Cataloging-in-Publication Data

Vaughn, Ellen Santilli.
    Time peace : living here and now with a timeless God / Ellen Vaughn.
       p.   cm.
    Includes bibliographical references.
    ISBN-13: 978-0-310-26726-3
    ISBN-10: 0-310-26726-9
    1. Time—Religious aspects—Christianity. 2. Time. I. Title.
  BT78.V38   2007
  231.7—dc22

                                                  2006039531

Published in association with the literary agency of Wolgemuth and Associates, Inc. 8600 Crestgate Circle, Orlando, FL 32819.

All Scripture quotations, unless otherwise indicated, are taken from the *Holy Bible: New International Version*®. NIV®. Copyright © 1973, 1978, 1984 by International Bible Society. Used by permission of Zondervan. All rights reserved.

Internet addresses (websites, blogs, etc.) and telephone numbers printed in this book are offered as a resource to you. These are not intended in any way to be or imply an endorsement on the part of Zondervan, nor do we vouch for the content of these sites and numbers for the life of this book.

Interior design by Beth Shagene

Printed in the United States of America

---

07 08 09 10 11 12 13 • 23 22 21 20 19 18 17 16 15 14 13 12 11 10 9 8 7 6 5 4 3 2 1

With great love to
Emily, Haley, and Walker,
my fellow time travelers
in the great Adventure

Contents

PART THREE

Re-Viewing Time:
A New Paradigm

PART FOUR

Enjoying Time

He has made everything beautiful in its time.

ECCLESIASTES

With Gratitude

I'm enormously grateful to the friends and family who helped to make this book possible. Andi Brindley and Walt and Diana Santilli shared their beautiful homes as writing retreats. Patti Bryce, Craig Falwell, Gail Harwood, Lee Vaughn, and Hugh Whelchel were kind enough to read the manuscript and give helpful feedback and critiques, as did Dr. Beverly Jamison and Dr. Jay Richards, whose insights and wit are both so brilliant. I thank Pat Macmillan for the opportunity to enjoy his incomparable brainstorming powers on the topic of time. I'm extremely grateful to Admiral Tim Ziemer and Connie Leachman for sharing their stories of God's faithfulness in times of great loss. Huge thanks to Norma Vaughn (Saint Norma) for her help with VaughnWorld at various junctures during the writing process.

I appreciate the prayer support of my sisters and brothers at McLean Presbyterian Church. I am grateful to my agent, Robert Wolgemuth, and Andrew and Erik Wolgemuth, for their solidarity and commitment to providing socks for the Vaughn youth. At Zondervan, John Sloan's creative insights and passion about writing and time made this project quite fun; thank you also to Bob Hudson for his editing excellence.

Thank you Emily, Haley, and Walker, for your flexibility regarding my writing schedule, and thank you for your enthusiasm for this book. And thank you, Lee, for your constant care and abiding love. I am glad we are partners in this journey through time. You are the best.

ELLEN VAUGHN
AUGUST, 2006

PART ONE

EXPERIENCING TIME

CHAPTER 1

Curiosity

ℓℐℴ

God has made everything beautiful for its own time.
He has planted eternity in the human heart,
but even so, people cannot see the whole scope
of God's work from beginning to end.[1]
ECCLESIASTES 3:11

My curiosity about time starts with three things.

The first has to do with how big God is and how small we are. People often say that Christianity is about a "relationship with God." True. But as I get older, I wonder: what does it really mean for a mortal being to have a "relationship" with One who dwells in eternity, who lives in cosmic dimensions beyond our conception?

How can a human biped, so trapped in time, really live in connection with a God who transcends it? How can His reality shape our own experience every day? What are we missing when we think only in terms of the here and now, so strapped to that watch on the wrist ... in the face of eternity?

The second issue that piques my curiosity about time is less cosmic and more practical. It has to do with how people experience time every day.

As I've polled others, I've found that many have a pretty negative feeling about time. Ask fifty people—random people who don't happen to believe in God—about their relationship with time, and most will sigh and roll their eyes. "Time? There's never enough of it!" They'll voice frustration, burnout, and guilt. Some will tell you how they wasted their best years in the past or how they worry about the future. Few will say that they're at peace with time.

Here's the rub: now ask fifty people—random people who *do* believe in God—the same question. If you catch them off guard, before they formulize the proper "spiritual" response, you'll get many of the same answers as from nonbelievers. For the most part, you'll hear the same stress, regret, and anxiety about time and its passage. Sadly, for many of us who are earnestly committed to Christ, this key perspective of everyday life is much like the vantage point of those who don't believe in Him.

If this is so, we're missing something vital, certainly in our experience, but also in our ability to demonstrate that God is real. Today many Christians are known for their political views or how they school their children or how they dress or talk. These are all fine things. But perhaps many of us are missing one of the most fundamental distinctions of real Christianity: *peace*. Is there a supernatural tranquility, joy, and freedom in the rhythms of our everyday lives, a heartbeat that is clearly not of this world? What *really* makes us tick? What motivates us from the inside out? Do we demonstrate, in everyday life, a *distinctive* relationship with time?

The third issue that intrigues me is how I am haunted, in a good way, by the words of Psalm 90. It's the oldest Psalm, written by Moses when he was old and his long white beard, parted like the Red Sea, fell to his waist. Moses contrasts God's eternal permanence with his own fleeting lifespan. He pleads with God, "Teach me to count my days! Satisfy us in the morning with your unfailing love, that we may ... be glad all our days!"

I'm like Moses, though I have no beard. Every morning I am more and more aware of the fact that my days are fleeting. The older I get, and the more I learn about God and His grace, the more I want to grab hold of His ankle, so to speak. Like Jacob wrestling with God in the Old Testament, I want to shout, "I won't let You go until You bless me! Teach me to count my days! Show me how to make them count, how to really live so that my days here on earth echo in eternity!"

So yes, I am curious about this thing we call time. So basic, yet so mysterious. How does an earth-bound person really connect with an eternal God? How can we really live with distinction, at peace in a culture so full of stress and "hurry sickness"? And how do we live our days in gladness and satisfaction, like Moses prayed, making them count?

I've queried all kinds of people about these things. Almost all have resonated with this issue of time. Not time *management*, but how to grab the ankle of this most elusive and familiar element of our lives. The arrow of time hits a tender mark in the human heart; we long to be at peace with its passage. For most of us, such peace would be absolutely radical and life-changing.

This book thus grew out of curiosity, conversations, and my own growing convictions about a refreshed approach to time. Clearly it's not a definitive study of such an enormous topic. But I hope it will take the reader, as it has me, on a journey of wonder, toward the end of newly discovering the God who is so far beyond us ... and yet somehow too so close.

CHAPTER 2

Wonder

Nothing is too wonderful to be true.
Michael Faraday

*Secularism, materialism, and the intrusive presence of things have put out
the light in our souls and turned us into a generation of zombies.
We cover our deep ignorance with words, but we are ashamed to wonder,
we are afraid to whisper 'mystery.'[1]*
A. W. Tozer

God's "beyondness" is unmistakable. Compared to Him, we are so small. His life is eternal, no beginning or end. Ours is fleeting, so brief in time.

Yet even in our limitations, we can know Him. He has scattered evidence of His magnificence throughout the universe, in the heights of the heavens and the invisible depths of the atom.

On clear winter nights, when we stare at the constellation Orion, we crane our necks with the same upward wonder as the ancients who first saw in this star-pattern a mighty hunter. We're somehow linked with 2000 B.C. Job, shivering in a robe, staring in our smallness at the distant stars. For his part, Job said,

> [God] is the Maker of the Bear and Orion,
> the Pleiades and the constellations of the south.
>
> He performs wonders that cannot be fathomed,
> miracles that cannot be counted.[2]

Job's appreciation of the miraculous would have been multiplied if he had today's tools.

Modern telescopes tell us that Betelgeuse, that bright star in Orion's shoulder, is 3,000,000,000,000,000 — three quadrillion — miles away. It is 400 million miles wide, a violently roiling red inferno with a froth of fire casually flung like a scarf that streams ten million miles into space.

How big is the Being who made this thing? How vast is His measureless eternity?

We cannot conceive of the enormity.

Look at the constellation Andromeda. The Greeks named her after a mythical princess. She is home to an enormous spiral galaxy much like our own. And the distance to her? Here's where our perspective on time must stretch, for we see Andromeda not as she is now, but as she was two and a half million years ago. That's how long it takes for her light to reach our earth. If we climbed aboard a 747 and traveled at conventional airline speed — wearing some very warm clothes and a major oxygen mask — it would take two trillion years to reach her.

Yet God is above and beyond such time.

Take things the opposite direction, from the macro to the micro.

The dot on this *i* holds 500,000,000,000 particles of matter called protons. If you compressed one proton down to a billionth of its normal size, the spot that is left has no appreciable dimensions. It's called a singularity. In mathematics, this term describes something that is patently indefinable, like 1/0. The notion of the "present" is similarly uncooperative: as soon as we say, "This is now!" it is gone. Though we talk about it all the time, the present does not really exist.

Now, moving to astrophysics, imagine all the stuff of the entire universe — the matter of galaxies, stars, planets, everything — packed into that inestimably small singularity. Then try to envision the explosive moment of creation. As writer Bill Bryson says, you'll want to retire to a safe place to observe the spectacle. Unfortunately, there is no safe place, because there is no *where*. No space. No time. From nothing, the universe begins.

Bryson writes, "In a single blinding pulse, a moment of glory much too swift and expansive for any form of words, the singularity assumes heavenly dimensions, space beyond conception. In less than a minute the universe is a million billion miles across and growing fast ..."[3]

It's not my intention here to present a case for God as the Creator of this beginning, in order to try to convince readers who don't hold that point of view. Many experts have written winsomely, cogently, and comprehensively about the questions of origins and the evidence that One outside the universe made it and everything in it. My aim in this book is to consider the nature of what God has made, what such wonders show us about *His* nature and how God's eternity can inform and transform human beings' experience in time.

Scientific discovery can be metaphorical: its physical truths point to spiritual realities that are far more grand. Creation's majestic wonders give a glimpse of the glory of the Creator who made them. Cosmology's natural phenomena, particularly as they relate to time, point to even grander *super*natural marvels and mysteries. They create awe, even holy fear at the unapproachable vastness of the mind of God. We're left shaking our heads, humbled. How could One so huge possibly care about us?

Then comes the impossible part. This grand, unreachable God came to us.

The Bible says that in the "fullness of time" Jesus Christ came to earth. The Incarnation means that the Creator of the cosmos arrived on the planet—a blue marble in a universe ten billion light-years in diameter. He came in a human body ... to a small town ... as an infant.

Like a reverse Big Bang, the limitless God, the eternal super-intelligence beyond reckoning, compacted Himself into a six-pound swaddled bundle. He chose to subject Himself to the passage of earth-time, with its weariness, aging, longing, and death. Jesus lived in time ... but His perspective was that of eternity.

What on earth can this mean for us?

There are tons of books about managing time, maximizing it, controlling it, organizing it ... all toward the end of greater efficiency, less stress, better time management, less tooth decay. While these are important issues and we are all for healthy teeth, these are not ends in and of themselves. Perhaps the emphasis today on "managing" time has suppressed our ability to wonder. Perhaps our preoccupation with practicality has compressed our vision, as if human experience is as narrow as a pocket calendar, and God is but a celestial accountant. For the believer, a new experience of time is not dependent on managing it better. As we'll see, it depends on developing a mind-blowing new paradigm altogether.

In addition to books about time management, there are also many specialized scientific tomes about time and eternity. There are reams of physicists' papers on special and general relativity, the space-time continuum, quantum mechanics, and string theory. Most of them are incomprehensible to those of us who don't have advanced degrees in physics.

The story is told of a Russian poet visiting London before the First World War. He got lost and was running late to an appointment. In his broken English, he asked a man on the street, "Please, sir, what is time?"

"But that's a philosophical question!" the man replied. "Why ask me?"

He's right, and there are hefty stacks of philosophical discussions about the nature of time as it relates to the nature of God. Christian philosophers take the fundamentals regarding what Scripture says about God and time, and arrive at different philosophical conclusions. Does God dwell in "divine timeless eternity" or "timelessness and omnitemporality" or "unqualified divine temporality"? Or "relative timelessness"?[4]

We don't know.

What we do know is that God is far beyond our own experience. Eternity is more than we can comprehend. It is good to cultivate awe and wonder about such mysteries ... because how we think about time, use time, and have peace in time—or not—depends on how we really think about God.

How big is He? Do we trust Him, really? Do we believe that He has given us "enough" time?

If we believe what we say we do—in a huge, sovereign, good God who created all things, including time, and has ordained both our days on earth and our entrance into eternity—we will not be anxious about time. We are in fact rich in it. We can enjoy God's present. We can relax, and smile.

꙰

Parts of this book point to the grand vistas of cosmology, astronomy, physics, and what science's theater can show us about the nature of God, time, and eternity. His wondrous enormity makes all the more eccentric His decision to cultivate, at great cost, relationships with mere human beings.

I'm no rocket scientist. Scientists themselves affirm that physics, on both the macro and the micro levels, is a field in which many understand nothing and none understands everything.[5]

But discoveries about the natural world reveal some of God's invisible qualities ... His eternal power and divine nature, so different from ours. Exploring the starry fields of His creation causes us to live on the edge of wonder. It scratches at a deep-down, curious itch. It assuages the sadness we sense when time slips so quickly away. It acknowledges the longing for eternity that is planted deep within our hearts. It makes us hungry for heaven in a way that helps us live better on earth.

Thus another part of this book is like any good Martha. It puts its hands on its hips, wearing an apron, and responds to the stargazing sections: "So what? Anyway, it's time for dinner!"

Well, dinner is good. And the great thing about grand truths is that they are not esoteric factoids existing in a vacuum somewhere. Truth has practical consequences in everyday life. For example, when people first realized the earth was not flat, but round, that information had effects in their daily lives. For one, they no longer had to live in fear of falling off the edge and could thus go on cruises with confidence.

For me, touching—ever so lightly—on the astounding nature of time, the universe, and the reality of God's great weight of glory stirs a new sense of wonder, awakening worship. These explorations also bring home the same thing that we tell our children: "It's not all about us." We're too small. This does not diminish our significance. Just our self-importance. Considering God's grandeur puts our time into the right perspective, widening the frame of days that have gone too narrow.

To borrow from Charles Spurgeon, "They who navigate little streams and shallow creeks, know but little of the God of tempests; but they who 'do business in the great waters,' these see His 'wonders in the deep.' Among the huge Atlantic-waves ... we learn the power of Jehovah, because we feel the littleness of man."[6]

The truths of God's great deeps, unfathomable as they are, lift our sights from the commonplace. At the same time, because God intimately cares about every hour of our lives and every hair on our heads, His glory can infuse every ordinary day we get to live down here.

Thus the echoes of the Big Beginning and the unspooling of time lure us to worship the Creator who flung everything into existence, to sense our own smallness, and to both fear and trust in One so huge. In turn, we can release small fears and worries. We can savor each little earth-day we are given, and live with purpose, even a sense of legacy ... for what we do in this life echoes in eternity, in ways we cannot understand until we arrive there. Wherever *there* is.

CHAPTER 3

Time Flies

∽⊙∽

For I have known them all already, known them all:
Have known the evenings, mornings, afternoons,
I have measured out my life with coffee spoons . . .
T. S. ELIOT, FROM
"THE LOVE SONG OF J. ALFRED PRUFROCK"

It is indeed grand to contemplate the wonders of time and eternity.

But most of us live in an everyday frenzy where we just don't stop to think about these things. Perhaps our most prevalent thought about the nature of time is simply this: time flies.

I was hit with this fact in a fresh way during a large-scale attack on my hometown.

The assault on Washington came in late spring. The terror alert was elevated. D. C. citizens had even been warned as to the time, place, and means of the invasion.

Yet we were helpless in the face of the onslaught. Boldly premeditated, flawlessly synchronized, it paralyzed the capitol city and its suburbs. Red-eyed, relentless, and suicidal, the attackers invaded schoolyards, churches, synagogues, mosques, and neighborhoods with impunity. They made no distinction between combatants and civilians, old and young. Burrowing up from hidden underground bunkers at sunset, billions of cicadas marched on Washington.

It is useful to study one's enemy. These cicadas are flying, plant-sucking insects that incubate underground. They emerge every seventeen years, precisely, to eat, drink, and be merry for a few short weeks. They mate, lay eggs, and die. An inch and a half long, they have black bodies, orange wing veins, and extra-terrestrial-style red eyes.

This particular cicada infestation, known as Brood X, emerged from the ground at the rate of 1.5 million per acre. Then they began their mating calls.

Experts informed concerned citizens that male cicadas have a pair of tymbals, or ridged membranes, on their first abdominal segment. The abdomen is hollow and acts as a resonating chamber. Driven mad by their hormones, males climbed to sunlit branches, arranged themselves in "choruses," and amorously commenced hitting their tymbals.

The resulting noise was absolutely deafening. People wore earplugs when they went out to get their morning newspapers. We could not hold conversations outside, though now and then we would venture into the yard with the phone held up, so friends in other states could hear the unbelievable, alien din.

Early on in the invasion, I headed out one morning. The spring breeze lifted my hair as I stepped down from my porch, balancing a folder of papers, car keys, and a travel mug. Running late, I swung into our Suburban's driver's seat and backed out of the driveway, coffee in hand.

A huge, ungainly bug, flying in erratic circles, buzzed in my open window, its red eyes crazed as if it wanted to mate with me. Emitting strange chittering sounds just like the little dinosaurs in "Jurassic Park," it landed in my hair. Its feet had little claws. It bumbled further down, heading toward my mouth. I screamed, spilled coffee everywhere, and drove into the mailbox.

I was not alone. The cicadas wreaked havoc on traffic. The local media reported pile-ups on the Capitol Beltway, crashes in neighborhoods, angry convertible owners with their tops zipped tight.

Meanwhile, hundreds of local couples had earnestly planned their weddings for late May, unaware of the impending invasion. They were in conniptions. Outdoor catered events looked like the sets of Japanese horror movies. The cicadas crash-landed in food trays, crawled on wedding cakes, died in champagne glasses. They clung to every leaf and flower, littered the sidewalks, crunched in the fresh spring grass. Random wings, antennae, and exoskeletons were every-where. Brides wore their veils down; their grooms brandished enor-mous fly swatters tied with silk ribbons.

Accordingly, there was a four hundred percent increase in tent rentals. Outdoor parties imported huge structures with strong sides, armored flaps, and thick flooring.

Some residents fought back by eating the invaders. News report-ers appeared with local chefs and plates of cicadas, lightly battered and deep-fried, with marinara sauce on the side, or simply sautéed in butter and garlic. A pastry chef froze the bugs and then coated them in fine chocolate for cake decorations.

Our dog did his part, gulping down hundreds of the protein-rich little suckers every day. But they could not be eaten away. "Popu-lation densities are so high that predators apparently eat their fill without significantly reducing the numbers," the cicada experts told us. "This is known as predator satiation."

Eventually, however, they began to die of their own accord. One and a half million per square acre, give or take a few dog mouthfuls, lay deceased and decaying on the ground, in trees, everywhere. The stench was incredible.

As I settled into bed one night, earplugs and nose plugs in place, I thought about the bugs. I remembered my first experience with a ci-cada invasion, back when I was in junior high. My friends and I had fastened little lassos to their abdomens. Like cowboys at a rodeo, we held them as they buzzed in circles around our heads. I thought about the uncanny precision with which the cicadas appeared .... every seventeen years. What an incredibly reliable cycle of life! Amazing, I mused. And let's see, how old will I be when these beetles return?

Suddenly I sat bolt upright, shocked. Sixty-four! Impossible. Sixty-four? The Beatles—appropriately—began singing in my brain, "Will you still need me, will you still feed me, when I'm sixty-four?"

Suddenly I saw my life streaming by like a fast-flowing river, measured out not by coffee spoons, like J. Alfred Prufrock's, but by seventeen-year increments of cicada development. How many times, total, would I see these things? Maybe five times in a lifetime?

Only five?

The cicadas' life span seemed so short, a few springtime weeks before they withered and died. But clearly my own span was not so grand. Before I know it, I thought, my hair will be wiry-gray, coiffed in a grandma-do. My blue-veined hands will swat away at Son of Bug, Brood X^2 ··· I'll miss and tumble on the lawn in a heap: "I've fallen, and I can't get up!"

Well. Such overwrought thoughts are the stuff of sleepless nights, when the mind wanders down dark hallways, jiggling at the knobs of random doors. But even at high noon, it's hard to ignore the runaway train of time. It goes so fast.

CHAPTER 4

Time Hurts

~ళ్ళు~

Sunrise, sunset . . . Swiftly fly the years
One season following another
Laden with happiness and tears.
FIDDLER ON THE ROOF

Time is but the stream I go a-fishing in.
I drink at it; but while I drink I see the sandy bottom
and detect how shallow it is.
Its thin current slides away, but eternity remains.
I would drink deeper;
fish in the sky whose bottom is pebbly with stars.
HENRY DAVID THOREAU

"But at my back I always hear / Time's wingèd chariot hurrying near," wrote seventeenth-century poet Andrew Marvell. I feel it too. The wheels turn, turn, turn, churning the dust. The dry sand runs through the glass. Seasons pass. Flowers grow; they wither and fade. Children, once toddlers, turn into teens. Parents die. Icons age. Opie has been bald for years. Time's passage is inevitable, inexorable, inescapable. Yet it's still shocking. It tears at us with a rupturing, poignant sense of sadness.

I once said this to a friend without further explanation, assuming that everyone felt the same way. He looked at me with his eyebrows up, needing more definition. "But what do you mean?" he asked.

I envy his pain-free stance. But many of us do feel time's shadow of sadness. At the end of the day, when twilight comes, a twinge of loss comes as well. Another day is done, and our brain chemistry is sad about it.

When life draws still and we feel the thudding of our hearts, we wonder when that beat will stop. We mourn a little to see the fresh flower that will droop so soon, the child who will eventually drive off to college without a backward glance, the once-capable parent whom we now tend. Time flies. It hurts.

Mundane daily stresses stir only the surface of our lives. Down in the deep waters near the heart, profound things throb. They come in the dark of the night, in life's sad farewells, and even in the sweet richness of its celebrations. The toasts of the wedding feast speak of glad new beginnings, but they signal endings too. Graduations are not just the happy toss of a tasseled hat, but a step through a one-way door. The beauty of the sunset breaks my heart; so soon it fades away. Beauty hurts because it passes. Immutable Beauty awaits, but we do not see it yet. And here in the shadow-lands, life's spool unwinds. Its strands are golden and dark, heavy and light. The wheel won't stop. There is no rewind, no redo. No second draft.

Philosopher William Craig writes about reading to his children from Laura Ingalls Wilder's classic *Little House in the Big Woods*. The Ingalls girls are drowsing by the fireplace one winter night, listening to their father play his fiddle, his "strong, sweet voice softly singing 'Auld Lang Syne.'"

"What are days of auld lang syne, Pa?" Laura calls to her dad.

"They are days of a long time ago, Laura," her father replies.

Laura listens to her father's fiddle "softly playing and to the lonely sound of the wind in the Big Woods. She looked at Pa sitting on the bench by the hearth, the firelight gleaming on his brown hair and beard and glistening on the honey-brown fiddle. She looked at Ma, gently rocking and knitting."

"She thought to herself, 'This is now.'"

"She was glad that the cozy house, and Pa and Ma and the firelight and the music, were now. They could not be forgotten, she thought, because now is now. It can never be a long time ago."[1]

This passage is so poignant, says William Craig, because we read it and know that Laura's "now" is gone forever.[2] It's the same for us. Any golden moment by the fire is gone in a flash. Our lives so "quickly pass, and we fly away," as Moses put it.[3]

I remember a "this is now" moment, sitting in the last class of senior year of high school, jotting on the last page of a notebook as I waited for the last bell.

Time seemed suspended. There were the faces of my friends, just like always. I breathed in the familiar school smell—that mix of pencils, people, and peanut butter. There was the yearbook, with its neat rows of faces and scribbled signatures. Same as ever. But once that final bell tolled, it would all be over. We would scatter to summer jobs, then away from home and off to college, never to be in high school again.

I remember one who did not graduate with us. Doug was a classmate who was attacked and brutally beaten when we were sophomores. For several days he had hovered in a nether place, on life support in our local hospital's intensive care unit. I worked in that hospital's laboratory office after school. Part of my job was to deliver patients' lab reports to the nursing stations. On my rounds each day, I would creep into the ICU and drop off the papers. Then I'd peek over at the curled heap on the narrow bed; Doug was barely visible amid all the bandages, tubes and wires. He was fifteen, my age. Then the machines were turned off, and time stopped for him, right there. Fifteen forever?

I remember a still point years earlier, when I was about ten. It was September 1. I was visiting an elderly lady who cultivated a large garden. The skies were endless blue. As I walked in the green grass among the late-summer blooms of red and gold, the briefness of such beauty suddenly hit me. Soon dark clouds and cold winds would come, and the garden would fade to gray. It made me sad. I wanted to hold onto that moment, full of beauty. But of course I couldn't.

These are the longings of a thousand songs. "Forever young," sang rocker Rod Stewart. "... in my heart you will remain, forever young." Rod's now in his sixties. Singer Jim Croce had a similar thought. "If I could put time in a bottle," he sang hauntingly,

The first thing that I'd like to do,
Is to save every day
'Til eternity passes away,
Just to spend them with you.

But there never seems to be enough time....

Jim Croce happened to share Rod Stewart's birthday—but *he* never got to his sixties. Killed in a plane crash in 1973, he is forever thirty. Forever young.

A number of plastic surgery centers use Stewart's phrase in their promotional brochures. "Forever young!" they advertise cheerfully, as if it is possible. Suctioning, nipping, tucking, peeling, buffing, fluffing—all are energetic attempts, surely, to fight gravity's drooping pull. But they won't stop the march of time.

As another lyric puts it:

Time can tear down a building or destroy a woman's face
Hours are like diamonds, don't let them waste

Time waits for no one, no favors has he
Time waits for no one, and he won't wait for me.

So sang the Rolling Stones in 1973, back when Mick Jagger and Keith Richards were young and wild. They were right. Time didn't wait, and now they're grandfathers.

The same thing has happened to me. Not that I'm a grandfather. But as I get older, life gets stranger. Now when I put my arm through a shirt sleeve, my mother's hand pops out. What's that about? My peers are middle-aged, but we are all much younger than middle-aged people used to be when I was twenty.

No one, Rolling Stone or ancient philosopher or modern person on the street, would argue that time is not fleeting. When we stay still for a moment and confront the truth, life is short. We age so quickly. Time flies. Its passage hurts. It waits for no one.

The question is, what do we *do* in the face of that fact? Do we try to deny it, control it, medicate the pain of life's quick trip? Do we seize the day, grab for the gusto, eat, drink, and be merry while we can, like big cicadas, beating our tymbals and mating wildly?

To consider all this, it's helpful to look at one of the most dramatic chapters in human history.

CHAPTER 5

Haven't Got Time for the Pain

~⊙~

One should always be drunk.
That's the great thing; the only question.
Not to feel the horrible burden of Time
weighing on your shoulders and bowing you to the earth,
you should be drunk without respite. Drunk with what?
With wine, with poetry, or with virtue, as you please.
CHARLES BAUDELAIRE, *PARIS SPLEEN*, 1869

On a clear October day in 1347, twelve ships put into the port of Messina, Sicily. Nothing seemed unusual about the vessels. A light wind blew. Fishermen unloaded their catch, and fish flopped on the wooden dock. Children played on the sand below. Merchants called to their customers.

The ships' anchors dropped. Their gangplanks lowered ... and then a few sweating, dying sailors staggered onto the dock. Their blackened skin stretched over bloody, egg-sized mounds — the trademark boils of plague. They coughed, moaned, and fell to their knees.

People screamed, scattered, and normal life stopped.

The ships were expelled, the dead and dying dumped in the sea. But it was too late. A highly contagious, adaptable pathogen called *Y pestis* was already loose in Sicily, carried by fleas that attached themselves to rats, then humans. A variation of the disease attacked the respiratory system; exhaled by one person, it was inhaled by another. And another. Exponentially. Bubonic and pneumonic plagues were unleashed on Europe.

The Black Death, as it came to be called, killed millions. Europe lost a third of its population in some areas, 60 percent in others. In the Islamic Middle East and North Africa about a third of the inhabitants died, in China almost half. Today a demographic disaster on the scale of the Black Death would claim about 1.9 billion lives.[1]

Writings from those terrible days read like accounts of the end of the world. Men and women died in their houses, in the streets, their bodies layered "like lasagna" in stinking burial pits.

There were not enough coffins, not enough graves. Whole towns emptied of the living and were filled with the dead. Feral dogs and snarling pigs chewed on corpses in the streets. Moaning, weeping, and the babbling delusions of the dying filled the nights. People went mad with the horror.

Children died as well, by the millions. Some say that the plague became part of their play, a dark rhyme they sang as they danced in circles, chanting about the rose-colored plague boils, the flowers people carried in a vain attempt to ward off infection, and the end of it all, when everyone they knew fell down to die:

> *Ring around the rosie*
> *Pocket full of posies*
> *Ashes, ashes:*
> *We all fall down.*

Then came the silence. "By the time the pestilence ended, vast stretches of the inhabited world had fallen silent, except for the sound of the wind rustling through the empty, overgrown fields."[2]

Plague aside, life was already brief and violent in those medieval days. If people weren't killed by "normal" diseases, marauding warriors, accidents, or domestic quarrels, most common folk died of old age, worn out and toothless, by thirty. But the Great Mortality, or the Year of Annihilation, as it was called in Muslim lands, brought death's grim reaper to every door.

So the residents of Europe and Asia during the Black Death were very aware of time's relentless march. Their behaviors thus show a highly concentrated picture of the fundamental human responses to the passage of time and the certainty of death.

Some took control and killed themselves before they could be ravaged by plague.

Some took solace in real Christianity, identifying more closely with the sufferings of Jesus. They reasoned that God could raise them, like Christ, to new life beyond the grave. They nursed the sick, comforted the dying, and passed on in peace in spite of the horror.

Some missed the Gospel and relied instead on the warped religiosity of their day. They bargained with God: if they gave more to the Church, perhaps they'd be spared. Orders of flagellants traveled from town to town, beating themselves with leather whips and calling others to shame and self-punishment that might satisfy God's wrath.

Some looked for scapegoats. Blaming the plague on "Christ-killers," they set upon Jews, dragged them out of their houses, and burned them in the public squares. Thousands of Jews were killed as these pogroms blazed across Europe.

And some raged against the absurd terror of it all, reasoning that there was no God, or at any rate He had abandoned them. The only recourse was to live for the moment, for tomorrow—or later today—they would die. The medieval writer Boccaccio records that some people "thought the sure cure for the plague was to drink and be merry, to go about ... amusing themselves, satisfying every appetite they could, drinking all day and night.... People behaved as though their days were numbered and treated their belongings and own persons with abandon."[3]

At dinner parties in plague-ravaged Florence, conversations were restricted to upbeat topics; the doors were barred against the living dead just outside. Meanwhile, naked men and women coupled on freshly dug graves, defying death even as they lay entwined in its reeking bed.

Certainly our modern world has horrors of every kind—terrorism, tsunamis, hurricanes, disease, murders. Scientists say that we are overdue for a pandemic of catastrophic proportions; avian flu and other threats cloud our horizons. Yet we have not yet experienced the overwhelming reality of life's fragility and time's passing as did the citizens of fourteenth century Europe and Asia.

Today, in First-World countries, our very comforts shield and anesthetize us from death in a way that our medieval friends could only have dreamed. Our distractions keep our fears at bay. We don't tend to think about death unless it penetrates our force-fields and affects us directly. We don't like to think that there's nothing we can do to slow time's passage.

Psychologists say that the normal human reaction to feelings of helplessness and vulnerability is the need to gain control. Americans, in particular, have always had control issues; part of our national identity is the desire to order our environment, government, and culture in ways that affirm our freedoms and our individuality.

So we try to control the passage of time.

For example, grandmothers today don't get old. They use a spectrum of body care products that "defy the effects of time," if the "age-defying" website they buy from is to be believed. Today's grandmas go to the gym in spandex, own a juicer, and have line-free Botox brows. They're perky. They don't have gray buns or carry any extra weight like the aproned matriarchs of yesteryear, who stayed at home, made yeasty dinner rolls, and used words like "yesteryear." Grandad works out too; he drives a neat little convertible and just got back from yoga class. Even if Grandma, who goes by Ann, did make dinner rolls, he couldn't eat them, because he's on the South Beach diet and can only have a little salad, no dressing, and a piece of grilled salmon the size of a cell phone.

Today not too many Americans fornicate in cemeteries like the people during the days of the plague. But maybe, in today's sex-soaked pop culture, perhaps there is an unconscious belief that sex *will*, somehow, stave off death. At least it distracts human beings from their inevitable departure. It's a user-friendly form of denial.

We see it in the clichés of the midlife crisis, which have become clichés only because they happen so often. Panicked by the relentless march of time that lines his face and puffs his paunch, the middle-aged man buys a red sports car and trades in his wife for a newer model. Somehow, having an affair with a younger woman makes him feel young again. Aging and death don't seem so real. Some women do the same thing, running off with the fitness instructor or the work colleague or the choir director.

The tidiest way to stem time's flood, though, is to escape. Many simply medicate the gnawing pain of time's passage.

The nineteenth-century French poet Charles Baudelaire wrote of this. It doesn't matter just *what* you use to blur your senses, he said ... just so you distract yourself from the throb of time's relentless passage.

Baudelaire followed his own advice, deadening time's sting with alcohol and opium until he died of his addictions and no longer had to worry about the pain of being alive. Millions of people do the same thing today, medicating themselves with whatever it takes—wine, work, food, drugs, sex, power, possessions, busyness, fame—to dull the pain of time's march and its ultimate end in the grave.

Albert Camus, Nobel-prize-winning writer of the last century, distilled the philosophical challenge facing those who don't believe in a personal God. Camus opened his book, *The Myth of Sisyphus*, with the cheery words, "There is but one truly philosophical problem, and that is suicide." One must decide whether or not to end one's pain as the days go by in a pointless universe.

For those who don't choose suicide, Camus used the Greek myth of Sisyphus as a parable for human heroism in the face of this meaninglessness. Sisyphus was condemned by the gods to roll a huge stone to the top of an enormous hill each day, only to have it roll back down to the bottom each evening. Endless, pointless, awful.

Camus writes of Sisyphus's effort,

> straining to raise the huge stone, to roll it and push it up a slope a hundred times over; one sees the face screwed up, the cheek tight against the stone, the shoulder bracing the clay-covered mass, the foot wedging it, the fresh start with arms outstretched ... At the very end of his long effort measured by skyless space and time without depth, the purpose is achieved. Then Sisyphus watches the stone rush down in a few moments toward that lower world whence he will have to push it up again toward the summit. He goes back down to the plain.[4]

This is a picture of human life, said Camus. It's a despairing picture. But it's a logical way to view life and the passage of time ... if there is no God who frames it all.

CHAPTER 6

Falling Ashes

Here, you see, it takes all the running
you can do to keep in the same place.
If you want to get somewhere else,
you must run at least twice as fast as that!
THE RED QUEEN IN
LEWIS CARROLL'S *ALICE IN WONDERLAND*

Even though Camus's choice of suicide or the perpetual, futile effort of Sisyphus sounds pretty grim, he did affirm those who hang in there in this gray realm of "skyless space and time without depth." Those who continue to live, validating their existence by action, are "absurd heroes." They know the extent of their ridiculous, hopeless condition, but they endure, disdaining their destiny. "There is no fate that cannot be surmounted by scorn," says Camus.[1]

A flamboyant example of one who said yes to Camus's question of suicide, and did pretty well with scorn as well, was the "gonzo" journalist Hunter S. Thompson. One of those larger-than-life characters who populate American letters from time to time, Thompson was famous for a writing style that blurred fact and fiction, one that fused the personality of the author with his subject matter. He smoked Dunhill cigarettes from a long holder, wore Tilly hats and white Converse sneakers, and consumed with abandon anything that would blur his own edges. "I hate to advocate drugs, alcohol, violence or insanity to anyone," he said, "but they've always worked for me."

He traveled extensively, wrote bestselling books about the Hell's Angels, the 1972 presidential election, and the underbelly of the

American dream, the aptly named *Fear and Loathing in Las Vegas*. He "cultivated the persona of a dangerously absurd, drug-crazed journalist bent on comic self-destruction."[2] He loved guns and lived in a heavily fortified compound in Colorado. Many years ago he ran for sheriff there on a "Freak Power" ticket. The conservative, incumbent sheriff had a crew cut; Thompson shaved his head bald and referred to the sheriff as "my long-haired opponent."

But by 2005, Hunter Thompson looked around and the fun was done. He was in poor health, in pain from hip-replacement surgery, depressed. He didn't want old age to dictate the circumstances of his death.[3] He had told a friend twenty-five years earlier that he would feel trapped if he didn't know he could commit suicide at any moment. Now, at sixty-seven years old, Thompson felt overdue to escape the trap.

One day he sat down with a black marker and wrote his last piece of journalism:

No More Games. No More Bombs. No More Walking. No More Fun. No More Swimming. That is 17 years past 50. 17 more than I needed or wanted. Boring. I am always bitchy. No Fun—for anybody. 67. You are getting Greedy. Act your old age. Relax—This won't hurt.[4]

Four days after penning that note, with his son, daughter-in-law, and grandson visiting for the weekend, Thompson was on the phone with his wife. He decisively concluded their conversation by sticking his 45 caliber pistol into his mouth and pulling the trigger.

Not to feel the horrible burden of time...

⸺

Six months after Hunter Thompson's suicide, friends gathered for his final farewell. Actor and Thompson friend Johnny Depp had funded a multi-million-dollar monument built in the shape of an enormous fist thrust into the sky. Defying the empty heavens, it featured a multicolored, blinking peyote button in its center. Based on Thompson's designs a few decades earlier, it stood two feet taller than the Statue of Liberty and looked like a "lighthouse on loan from Haight-Ashbury ... a bizarre hallucinogenic symbol soon to flicker out forever."[5]

The week before, Thompson's widow had delivered her husband's cremated remains to the Zambelli Fireworks company in Pennsylvania. Zambelli loaded Thompson's ashes into ten mortar shells packed with gunpowder. These were driven by armored car from Pennsylvania to Colorado and loaded into a cannon inside the towering, one-ton monument. People came from all over the country, including those who were not invited but camped on the hillsides to be near the festivities. "We just threw a gallon of Wild Turkey in the back and headed west," said one Thompson fan who drove 1,500 miles from West Virginia to pay his respects.[6]

Now, as the sun sank in the mountains and twilight fell, "Spirit in the Sky" began blasting over enormous loudspeakers. A friend read from a Tibetan sacred text. A troupe of Japanese drummers began a choreographed ritual. As the drumming stopped, echoing in the hills, champagne flutes were passed around. And then, in the silence, there was an enormous explosion as the cannon fired, the rocket soared into the darkness, and, as *Rolling Stone* reported, "Hunter's ashes fell over the assembled guests like gray snow ..."

The party began. It was an evening that would last until dawn, with the

> Gonzo fist in the sky and [Lyle] Lovett onstage singing 'If I Had a Pony' and raw oysters and Gonzo-emblazoned chocolates being handed out like Halloween candy ... with Bill Murray cutting a fine figure on the pavilion's dance floor and others serenading an inflatable sex doll until the sun finally rose and fatigue settled in and everybody drifted out of Owl Farm full as ticks from food and booze.[7]

As Thompson friend Douglas Brinkley left the proceedings, he wrote that suddenly a hush fell over the chartered bus that transported the partiers back to Aspen.

> You could hear the wheels humming down the lonesome Colorado blacktop road. Our transport had become as solemn as an empty church. No human murmurs or casual asides, just stony silence. As the highway turned sharply right, putting the phantasmagoric Gonzo fist out of view, the collective fear of everyone on board that we had all entered the No More Fun Zone.... The sorcerer was truly gone. [Thompson's] ashes had stilled, and only the dark shadow of the valley remained.[8]

Ashes, ashes, we all fall down.

⁓⊙⁓

In *The Great Mortality*, John Kelly writes that the medieval world woke one glorious morning to find the plague gone.

> Survivors drank intoxicatingly, fornicated wildly, spent lavishly, ate gluttonously, dressed extravagantly ... everywhere survivors luxuriated in the sudden abundance of a commodity that only a few months earlier had seemed so fragile, so perishable — *time*: wonderful, glorious, infinite time. Time for family, for work. Time to gaze into an evening sky. Time to eat and drink and make love."[9]

Time.
Some who had hoped that the black plague would spawn spiritual revival were disappointed. "It was thought," wrote one, "that people whom God by His grace in life had preserved ... would become better ... avoiding inequities and sins and overflowing with love and charity for one another. But ... the opposite happened. Men ... gave themselves over to the most disordered and sordid behavior." Another observer put it, "No one could restrain himself from doing anything."[10]

They had been given the gift of time, and they knew it.

The Black Death should have been enough to terrify and transform the toughest pagan. But the plague didn't really change people's views about time. How people responded to "wonderful, glorious time" depended on their character itself, not their experiences. As John Kelly puts it, "One thing even the Black Death could not change was human nature."[11]

In the end, people's fundamental beliefs—their worldview—determined their attitude toward time.

The same is true for those of us who live six and a half centuries later. How we experience time—so fleeting indeed—will depend on our real, deeply-held perspectives about God, life, death, and eternity.

CHAPTER 7

Devouring Beast
or Purring Pet?

[Time] is a version of the truth you wear on your wrist.
JAMES GLEICK, *FASTER*

You may say that not very many Christians are blasting their loved ones' ashes into outer space, raging against the existential absurdity of modern life, dancing with inflatable sex dolls, and tossing their empty bottles of booze into the woods.

That's only because you don't go to *my* church.

No, no, just kidding, you're right.

If the cosmos, time, and you and I came into existence through random chance over eons, then of course it doesn't matter how we use time: we have no intrinsic purpose and time doesn't either. Might as well eat, drink, and be merry, and put a bullet in the brain when the fun runs out.

But many of us have come to a different conclusion about the origins of life and time. The brilliant beauties and ordered complexity of the universe reveal a Designer. The visible wonders of the natural world disclose certain conclusions about the nature of this invisible One. As Romans puts it, "For since the creation of the world God's invisible qualities—his eternal power and divine nature—have been clearly seen, being understood from what has been made."[1]

But nature doesn't tell the whole story. "General revelation," as theologians put it, points to the glory of God ... but it doesn't reveal how in the world flawed and limited human beings can connect with this spectacular God.

This good news comes through "special" revelation: the Old and New Testaments, and the actual person of Christ. In Jesus, God came to earth as a human being, at a particular point in human time.[2]

Simply because He *is* love, this incredible God loves us. He came to save us from our wrongdoing and our limits. He gives the days of our lives meaning and purpose. His eternal limitlessness can make His people rich in time. He made it.

Time's succession of consecutive changes is what keeps everything from happening at once. Its sequential ordering of life is so much a part of us that we cannot conceive of existence without it.[3]

So we have to constantly remind ourselves that God the Father—more Alive than we can imagine, from everlasting to everlasting—exists, not in time like us, but in eternity. He is not bound by time. As C. S. Lewis described it,

> Our life comes to us moment by moment.... And of course you and I tend to take it for granted that this Time series—this arrangement of past, present and future—is not simply the way life comes to us, but the way that all things really exist. We tend to assume that the whole universe and God Himself are always moving on from past to future just as we do.... It was the Theologians who first started the idea that some things are not in Time at all; later the Philosophers took it over: and now some of the scientists are doing the same.[4]

When biblical writers describe God in terms of time-words, they refer to our time, not His. "Before the mountains were born or you brought forth the earth and the world, from everlasting to everlasting you are God," Moses wrote.[5] "The Lord is the true God; he is the living God, the eternal King," said Jeremiah.[6] When the apostle John saw a vision of God, living beings were crying out, "Holy, holy, holy is the Lord God Almighty, who *was*, and *is*, and *is to come*."[7]

These biblical phrases describe God by means of past, present, and future, since human tenses are our only option. This is appropriate

—at this point—because it's how God has chosen to reveal Himself to us. But God is uncreated, unchanging, unbound by time.[8]

Belief in this sovereign yet personal God can disarm philosophical angst about time. The reality of God's infinitude also has very practical ramifications. If God is really beyond the constraints of time, unhindered and unperplexed by it, then those who believe in Him can be free to live in absolute peace in time. We can be freed from time's chafing anxiety.

I love what the great old preacher A. W. Tozer said about this.

We poor human creatures are constantly being frustrated by limitations imposed upon us from without and within. The days of the years of our lives are few.... Life is a short and fevered rehearsal for a concert we cannot stay to give. Just when we appear to have attained some proficiency we are forced to lay our instruments down.

But there is hope!

How completely satisfying to turn from our limitations to a God who has none. Eternal years lie in His heart. For Him time does not pass, it remains; and *those who are in Christ share with Him all the riches of limitless time and endless years.*[9]

Incredible. In spite of its relentless quick passage, with its poignancy, pain, and pressure, time is not our enemy when we are friends with God. It is but a resource to be used, like food or oxygen. We can keep it, rather than be kept by it.

As Tozer says, with vivid metaphor, "For [non-believers], time is a devouring beast; before [believers] time crouches and purrs and licks their hands. The foe of the old human race becomes the friend of the new."[10]

Time can be tamed when we perceive its proper place in God's whole plan. Because God gives those who receive Him eternal life, our perspective of time can be radically different. The very limitlessness and infinitude of God can give His people an unearthly luxury of peace in time. God knows what will happen. His plans for us will end in good. He is in control. He gives us enough time every single day to do His will for that day. Every loving deed we do unto Him, every small thought we think to His glory, echoes in shimmering ripples throughout eternity.

We will look more at this enormously friendly and liberating idea in a few chapters. First, however, we need to set a bit more of the common context of the world in which we all live.

Dramatic examples like Hunter Thompson are not the norm. The norm in modern North American culture seems to be the route of quiet, rather than flamboyant, desperation. Madly multitasking, stressed and strapped, driven hither and thither, many Americans live in an outwardly productive but inwardly withering obsession with time. Many of the wonderful people we encounter every day — noble, unselfish, earnest people — struggle with this adversarial relationship with the clock.

Sociological studies show that the more advanced and wealthy a culture, the more likely its citizens are to think of time in economic terms. People in poorer countries tend to focus more on family and community than citizens of richer countries, who tend to focus more on the clock. Anxiety about time and schedules can shape our lives, narrow our relationships, and deaden our days.

This is the opposite of purring, friendly time. This is time as a beast. Though we would never consciously set out to do so, many worship at its altar. In First World cultures where people would never dream of bowing before a sacred tree or of leaving offerings for a carved image, time has become one of the most entrenched and insidious idols the world has ever seen, a roaring lion threatening to devour those who do not bring it proper sacrifices.

How did we become mechanized troops who march in lockstep to the click of the clock, a consumer culture consumed by the commodity of time, a people who worship at the drive-through altar of Our Lady of Perpetual Hurry? To find out, we need to look first at the colorful history of "keeping" time — a paradox, if there ever was one.

PART TWO

MANAGING TIME

CHAPTER 8

Keeping Time

Want to get the latest precision time keeping technology?...
Self-setting Atomic Travel Clock ...
will never lose or gain a second in one million years....
You can get this travel clock at the special introductory price of only $19.
At this low price they are going fast....

ODDLY WORDED AD IN *MILITARY OFFICER* MAGAZINE

Just off Massachusetts Avenue in Washington, D.C., the United States Naval Observatory is our nation's preeminent authority on the matter of time keeping. Its grounds are protected by elaborate security measures, in part because we don't want anyone to take our time, but also because the home of the vice president is on the same green hill of Washington real estate.

I first visited the Naval Observatory as a child. This was during the Cold War, when U.S. and Soviet tensions were high, when schoolchildren routinely practiced bomb drills in school. During these drills, loud alarms would sound and we would all dive under our little wooden desks. I don't remember even wondering how my little wooden desk would protect me from Soviet weapons of mass destruction.

At any rate, during this Observatory visit, I was about nine or ten years old. I was with my parents and a small group of adults, and our military host was explaining the inner workings of the facility as well as the functions of its large telescope, which was trained on galaxies far, far away from the dark skies of the Washington night.

It was past my bedtime, and the adults were craning their necks and staring at things too tall for me to grasp. Standing next to a stainless steel counter near the wall, I found that I was the exact height so that my chin was level with its surface. I was tired; in the way that children do, I stood facing the counter and rested my chin on top of it, closing my eyes and enjoying the feel of its smooth, cool surface.

After a while, I opened my eyes to move on. As I did, I became aware that without my realizing it, my small pointy child-chin had somehow pushed a recessed button located on the counter. I had the feeling that the Naval Observatory was not a place where buttons should be pushed frivolously. My heart jerked a little, and I casually ambled away, hands in my pockets, carefully looking as if my chin had not done anything wrong.

It had.

All activity in the observatory area abruptly ceased. Doors locked. The huge telescope froze in position. Alarms sounded. Troops snapped to full alert. The vice president was no doubt hustled away to a more secure location.

Odd as it seems, my child-sized chin had somehow found a lock-down control button in the United States Naval Observatory. And in my child-sized mind, I remember thinking that I had altered the course of the universe, or at least the destiny of the United States of America. I had stopped time.

My analysis overstated my power to change the course of anything. The Naval Observatory was back up and running very quickly. The Soviets did not attack. The vice president slept in his own bed that night. All was well.

Just recently, when I finally got over this childhood trauma, I tried to take my family to the Naval Observatory so our kids could take a tour. But security now is much tighter than it had been in my youth. Perhaps personnel there recognized me from their computer files of suspicious chins. Though master control buttons are no longer easily accessible to random children or adults, my requests for a tour went unanswered.

Among many other important tasks, the Naval Observatory keeps track of earth's rotation and maintains what is called Coordinated Universal Time. This is the adjusted time scale that forms the basis of civil time. Evidently the time ascertained by atomic clocks and that determined by the earth's natural rotation gets slightly out of synch. This is because the Earth's rotation is actually slowing down—in respect to the atomic clock time—due to the braking action of the ocean tides. The difference between the rotation clock and the atomic clock is about two milliseconds per day.[1]

But in order to keep things synchronized between the earth's rotational time and the more "absolute" atomic time, a leap second is added periodically—about every 500 days. Since we can't quite adjust the earth's rotation, we instead fine-tune the atomic clocks. This is the responsibility of the International Earth Rotation Service, whose name sounds very important.

The official United States time is determined at the Naval Observatory. Though milliseconds may not be particularly important to some of us, they make significant differences for modern electronic navigation and communications systems. Satellite positioning systems—used to navigate ships, planes, nuclear missiles, trucks, cars—are all based on the travel time of electromagnetic impulses. An accuracy of 10 nanoseconds (10 one-billionths of a second) corresponds to a position accuracy of about ten feet. So when you want to hit a threatening military target on the other side of the world, your clock had better be right.

Precise time measurements are also crucial for power companies, radio and television stations, and Super Bowl half-time shows, which all depend for their synchronization on the Naval Observatory Master Clock.

The Master Clock, which sounds like something out of *The Wizard of Oz*, resides, we presume, behind a massive velvet curtain from which smoke and awe pour forth. But it is actually not one clock but a measurement provided by sixty atomic clocks dwelling in separate, environmentally controlled vaults. These measure the microwave resonance frequency (9,192,631,770 cycles per second) of the cesium atom.

These atomic clocks are augmented by the big daddies, ten hydrogen maser atomic clocks, which also enjoy a pampered existence in environmentally controlled vaults, where federally funded workers bring them treats now and then. The Observatory automatically compares all these clocks every 100 seconds, computing a time scale that does not change by more than 100 picoseconds (.0000000001 seconds) per day. Thus, in Washington, any concerned citizen can dial 202–762–1401, and ask, "Please, sir, what is time?" and you will find out ... unless, of course, you are looking for a philosophical answer.

CHAPTER 9

From Sticks and Boxes
to Ion Clockses

‹ಀ›

New roads, new ruts.
G. K. CHESTERTON

Instant gratification takes too long.
CARRIE FISHER

The first devices to measure time were not up to the Naval Observatory's standard of precision. About 5,500 years ago, the Greeks discovered that a vertical post would cast a longer shadow when the sun was lower in the sky. These posts were called *gnomons*, from the Greek "to know." People could know the passage of time, and for the first time — on sunny days, at least — they could make appointments according to a common standard, as in "I'll meet you in front of my tent when the shadow is a hand's-breadth past the pole."

The Egyptians developed slightly more sophisticated T-bars and obelisks. Then came sundials, hourglasses, and water clocks.

Sociologist Robert Levine's excellent book, *A Geography of Time*, points out that the ancient Romans put a high value on time, their "time is money" mentality foreshadowing our own. Water clocks, or *clepsydrae*, were used in legal proceedings. There were many different types of such clocks; they all basically measured the amount of water that passed through a hole over a certain period.

So Roman lawyers would plead with judges for another water clock of time to present their client's case. *Aquam dare*, "to grant water," meant to give an attorney more time; *Aquam perdere*, "to lose water," meant to waste time. In the famed Roman senate, whenever a distinguished member went on and on in a long-winded speech, his colleagues would shout for "his water to be taken away."[1]

But water clocks clogged. Though still in use in parts of North Africa as late as the twentieth century, they just weren't particularly precise. Neither were similar inventions like ancient Chinese incense clocks or hour glasses or indexed candles. So human activities could be coordinated only loosely. Significant events had to be set for a time that people could commonly recognize—which is why so many duels, battles, and important meetings were held at dawn.

Benedictine monks, who gathered for set prayer times each day, needed a means to call their community together. So the ringing of the *clocca*, or bells, told the monks it was time to pray. They would amble in from the vegetable garden, the smell of rosemary hanging about their habits, as the beauty of the bells inclined their hearts toward God.

But *cloccas* eventually pushed people to new habits of pressure rather than prayer. As Carl Honore says in *In Praise of Slowness*, mechanical clocks soon ruled their owners' lives. The first public clock was probably erected in the German city of Cologne in around 1370. This would have been a weight-driven machine that was difficult to regulate and lost or gained minutes quite readily.

Nevertheless, in 1374 the town passed a statute that set the beginning and end of the workday and limited laborers' lunch break to "one hour and no longer." In 1391 the city set nighttime curfews. In the space of a generation, the people of Cologne went from never knowing for sure what time it was to allowing a clock to dictate when they worked, how long they took for lunch, and when they went home every night.[2]

By the early fifteenth century, smaller clocks were being made, and after the 1630s weight-driven timepieces called lantern clocks started to appear in upper-class homes.

One day in 1582 Galileo Galilei was sitting in a cathedral, watching a swinging lamp suspended by a long chain hanging from the lofty ceiling. Distracted from the homily, he noted that each swing was equal and had a natural rate of motion. Galileo was busy with other things for years, including a controversial argument about the structure of the universe and getting tried for heresy by the Inquisition. But eventually, in 1640, while under house arrest in a villa near Florence, he found a moment to design a pendulum clock, the result of the swaying lamp's inspiration so many years earlier.

Galileo died before he could complete his project, but the swinging Dutch scientist Christiaan Huygens picked up the pendulum and developed the first such clock in 1656.[3] The first prototypes, called "wags-on-the-wall," were hanging clocks. These were eventually encased in wood, made larger, and replaced by grandfather clocks.

At first these pendulum clocks were owned only by royalty. As their production costs decreased in the eighteenth century, they made their way into the homes of the well-to-do. The ability to "keep" time was a sign of status and privilege.

Still, the question was growing: were humans keeping time, or was time keeping them?

Gulliver's Travels captures the clock-centeredness of the increasingly commercial society. When Gulliver met the small inhabitants of Lilliput, they were not acquainted with the large, round, gold, ticking object he wore. "We conjecture it is either some unknown Animal, or the God that he worships.... But we are more inclined to the latter Opinion, because he assured us that he seldom did any Thing without consulting it ... and said it pointed out the Time for every Action of His Life."[4]

The human quest to keep track of time affected not only timepieces, of course, but calendars, which had been used in various forms since human beings first noted the movements of the heavenly bodies.

Five thousand years ago, Sumerians in what is now Iraq kept a calendar that divided the year into 30-day months. The ancient Egyptians devised a 365-day calendar based on the relationship of the star Sirius with the sun. Later the Christian Church fathers developed the Gregorian calendar, based on the motion of the earth around the sun.[5] The Hebrew calendar is lunisolar, its months set by lunar cycles, its years determined by solar cycles.

The Julian calendar was implemented by Julius Caesar in 46 B.C. It defined the year as having an average length of 365.25 days, with an extra day thrown in every four years.

But Caesar's calendar was off by about 11 minutes ... and by the sixteenth century, it was almost two weeks ahead of itself. In 1582, Pope Gregory XIII cut ten days out of October ... but this new "Gregorian" calendar applied only to lands over which the Catholic Church had dominion.

Later, grudgingly, most Protestant countries adopted the new calendar at the end of the seventeenth century, though England and its colonies did not switch until 1752. By the time they made this move, another bogus day from the Julian calendar had snuck into its citizens' lives. They were 11 days behind the rest of the world.

So by public caveat, September 2, 1752 was followed by September 14. Some people missed their birthdays. Others died and their families didn't know what date to put on their tombstones. Children were born 11 days older than they should have been. Workers rioted for missing wages. The time warp wreaked havoc with sensitive people's minds; a general malaise settled over those who just could not cope with the notion of days that had suddenly gone missing.[6]

Meanwhile, the clock-driven pace of life kept moving faster. The world lurched into overdrive with the Industrial Revolution. Engine power meant speed—people, information, and goods could travel across great distances faster than ever before. The business that churned its products out the fastest could reinvest for greater gain. "Time is money," said Benjamin Franklin, a formula taken to heart by Americans ever since.

Factories paid workers by the hour and accelerated output any way they could. People moved to cities, where they soon began to walk, talk, and work faster. Trains, subways, telegraphs, electric trams, cars, telephones, radios—the pace increased, invention by invention, churning toward the American dream of our own day: instant, global communications.

None of this growing need for speed could have been harnessed without accurate timekeeping. Though nineteenth century clocks were not reliable by today's standards, they set the parameters for factory workers' lives when punch clocks started being used in the late 1870s. When pocket watches and eventually wristwatches came along, they became a status symbol. The clock was perceived as a liberator, freeing people from the unreliable time measures they had used in the primitive past. Everyday language underscored the importance of this new invention: time was now, for the first time, "of the clock." As the phrase was shortened—since everyone was in a hurry—it became "o'clock."[7]

Appropriately, timepieces became smaller and smaller, moving closer and closer into people's personal space. Early on, as we've said, there were the public clocks of the city square. Then there were big grandfather clocks in every properly civilized home.

One day the great British writer G. K. Chesterton was barreling down a street in London, preoccupied with weighty thoughts, his thick cape flying behind him. As he turned a corner, head down, he collided with a man rolling a grandfather clock down the narrow sidewalk. Chesterton brushed himself off, scowled at the man, and shouted, "Why can't you just wear a wristwatch like everyone else?"

As timepieces got smaller—from grandfather clocks to wall clocks, table clocks, pocket watches—they became more and more a part of people's personal space. Wristwatches meant that people were constantly attached to the time, day and night. As one German cultural commentator put it, the wristwatch is "the handcuff of our time."[8] Today, clocks are a part of some people's very anatomy, in the form of the pacemaker.

Undergirded by the work ethic of the day, punctuality and productivity were held up as key virtues. A lesson in the 1881 edition of *McGuffey's Reader* darkly warned small children that tardiness could bring about "train crashes, failed businesses, military defeat, mistaken executions, thwarted romances: It is continually so in life, the best laid plans, the most important affairs, the fortunes of individuals, honor, happiness, life itself are daily sacrificed because somebody is behind time."[9]

Terrified that they might be inadvertently executed for being tardy, small turn-of-the-century Americans and Brits picked up the pace even more.

Today, for most of us, daily life runs at such a high rate of speed that we barely even notice it. The clock-centric culture is second nature to us now; it would be hard to conceive of a life without its pervasive pressure. We would be like fish out of water, our mouths in little *o*'s, confused, gasping for the quick current of hurry in which we swim.

~❦~

A few years ago, the National Institute of Standards and Technology used an atomic clock known as NIST-7, which won't gain or lose a second for a million years. The NIST-7, though, is now passé with the advent of the caesium fountain clock, which will keep perfect time, give or take a second, for fifteen million years. And soon that, too, will be only for slugs; scientists are working on a new form of time standard. It is called the ion trap, accurate to one second in ten billion years.

The problem with our modern obsession with time, though, is it seems that the ions aren't the only ones getting trapped.

CHAPTER 10

Nothing
Will Slow Us Down

No, no, Thursday won't work for me.
How about Never? Is Never good for you?

CARTOON

Just as Pavlov's dogs learned to salivate inappropriately,
we have learned to hurry inappropriately....
Our 'bells' have become the watch, the alarm clock, the morning coffee,
and the hundreds of self-inflicted expectations
that we build into our daily routine.
The subliminal message from the watch and the clock is:
time is running out; life is winding down; please hurry.

DR. LARRY DOSSEY,
SPACE, TIME AND MEDICINE

In the summer of 1998 Peggy Noonan wrote a prophetic essay for *Forbes ASAP* magazine. In it, the former presidential speechwriter mused about the nature of time in America's hurried culture.

"There is no such thing as time," Noonan began. "The past is gone and no longer exists, the future is an assumption that has not yet come, all you have is the moment—this one—but it too has passed ... just now."[1]

Noonan profiled the material blessings of our moment in history. We have such comforts, such ease with which we eat, drink, work, play, travel ... compared to "thousands of years of peasants eating rocks." Amazing. Yet there is no time to be amazed, for we are always in a hurry. "All our ... comfort takes time to pay for. And affluence wants to increase; it carries within it an unspoken command: More!"

So, said Noonan, we move faster to make more and get more and do more.

> So we work. The more you have, the more you need, the more you work and plan. This is odd in part because of all the spare time we should have. We don't, after all, have to haul water from the crick. We don't have to kill an antelope for dinner. I can microwave a Lean Cuisine in four minutes and eat it in five. I should have a lot of extra time — more, say, than a cavewoman. And yet I feel I do not.

> It's not just work ... work expands to fill the time allotted to complete it. This isn't new. But this is: So many of us feel we have no time to cook and serve a lovely three-course dinner, to write the long, thoughtful letter, to ever so patiently tutor the child. But other generations, not so long ago, did. And we have more timesaving devices than they did.

We have more conveniences than earlier generations, yet we seem to have less time. We have more of everything, yet so many are stressed and discontented. These paradoxes must end in some sort of resolution, wrote Noonan.

She sensed that something was coming, something that would cause people to stop and take stock. It wasn't an economic downturn, but something more sinister. In that summer of 1998, Noonan wrote of her fear that terrorists would strike the U.S., and that they would single out Manhattan, "where the economic and media power of the nation resides, the city that is the psychological center of our modernity, our hedonism, our creativity, our hard-shouldered hipness, our unthinking arrogance.

"If someone does the big, terrible thing to New York or Washington, there will be a lot of chaos ... and a lot of things won't be working so well anymore.... Something tells me we won't be teleconferencing.... Something tells me more of us will be praying, and hard, one side benefit of which is that there is sometimes a quality of stopped time when you pray. You get outside time."

Three years after Noonan wrote her provocative article, terrorists did do "the big, terrible thing to New York" and elsewhere. A week after the 9/11 attacks, the *Wall Street Journal* re-ran Noonan's visionary essay. Its insights were eerie indeed.

September 11 was a Black Plague moment. In its smoking ruins, life's brevity and priorities suddenly became clear. Americans realized anew the gift of time—wonderful, glorious time. It was a nation-wide wake-up call.

Many people did wake up. Many stopped their time-crunched rat race for "more" and instead pursued relationships with family, friends, and God. Many prayed hard. Many reassessed their lives and made significant changes for good. Many realized that life is not about excessive acquisition and consumption, but love and service.

But like the Black Plague, September 11 *itself* did not fundamentally change human nature. There was no great cultural shift in American life. Church attendance spiked right after the attacks but soon dropped back to pre 9/11 levels. Our national conversation today just does not seem to center on life's brevity, its blessings, the priority of family and friends. (And suffice it to say that pop culture doesn't spend much time pondering what really matters. Television, films, magazines, and the Internet don't celebrate the enduring spirit as much as they do the passing flesh ... and plenty of it. Talk shows don't feature loving, functional families, nor marriages that have deepened over decades. Wall Street and Capitol Hill don't seem to worry as much about helping the weak and needy as much as they do gaining and maintaining wealth and power.)

After all, September 11 didn't really shake what Noonan called America's economic and media power, nor our modernity, hedonism, or arrogance. We continue to pursue our love affair with affluence, with the perceived need for more and more, pursued and consumed ever faster and faster.

As we mentioned earlier, the seeds of this obsession with speed were planted in the Industrial Revolution: for the first time, people could move faster than a galloping horse, goods could be quickly mass-produced in the new factories; the spoils of commerce went to the fastest manufacturer. Money and time were linked.

The new technologies of the Industrial Revolution, like the incredible developments in our own day, were in large part wonderful advancements. The speed-enhancing devices of the 1800s helped give rise to the West's economic growth and the wealth it enjoys today. The prosperity generated by the efficiency of the new inventions of the day also made it possible for millions of people to live much longer. Human beings' God-given creativity can generate tools with potential for enormous good.

But the problem is, our speedy technologies often become masters rather than tools. We can become addicted with speed for speed's sake and lose touch with anything that is time-consuming. Like relationships.

Today, in more developed nations, people refer to time in economic terms, as in "spending" it, "saving" it, and "leveraging" it. Wealthy countries tend to be "time poor," their citizens typically feeling that they don't have enough of it. Economically poorer nations tend to be "time rich." Their inhabitants don't tend to be stressed by the tick of the clock; they are more relationship-centered than clock-centered.

I saw this a few months ago in the Amazon jungle. I was there with a friend who has devoted both his fortune and his time to building churches, schools, and orphanages in poor nations. After riding in small pickup trucks over dangerous jungle roads (with gun-toting guards standing in the back to protect us from armed robbers), we arrived at a small village in northern Peru. We heard singing and clapping. Schoolchildren, curious villagers, and believers dressed in ceremonial Quechua costumes were all waiting to welcome us.

They took us to the new church they had built. We worshiped God together for a few hours, and then it was time to eat. Our hosts had slaughtered a bull in honor of the occasion; he had been cooking in a big pit for quite a long time. There were huge pots of steaming rice and mounds of mangoes, papayas, and pineapples, pulled that morning from the earth. Children played. Dogs and random pigs came and went. Grandmas held babies on their knees.

Surely we enjoy great picnics and parties in the U.S. But there was a different quality to this occasion. Our Peruvian friends were fully in the moment. No one had to scoot out early because of a schedule conflict. No one was on a cell phone, or a Blackberry, multi-tasking during the meal. Everyone was relishing the feast.

After all, this roasted beast was a rare pleasure. They had anticipated it for a long time. After this day had passed, they would savor the memory—not because we were so wonderful, but because they truly valued relationships in a way that affluent people sometimes do not. Some of our "feasts" in the U.S. have lost their celebratory quality because we are too busy to anticipate them, too full to hunger for them, and too harried to remember them.

As Carl Honore put it after a long study of the hurried North American lifestyle, "We have forgotten how to look forward to things, and how to enjoy the moment when they arrive. Restaurants report that hurried diners increasingly pay the bill and order a taxi while eating dessert. Many fans leave sporting events early, no matter how close the score is,"[2] simply to avoid the traffic and get home faster . . . presumably so they can check their email and surf the Internet in order to find out how the game ended.

Does all this mean we have to be poor to have good relationships? No. It was, in fact, my friend's wealth that had enabled him to help the people in the Peruvian village. Because he is spiritually centered and perceives himself a steward of *God's* money and *God's* time, he is one of the most generous, loving, and time-efficient people I know. Wealth and time-saving technology, of course, don't preclude relationships. They just amplify the need for us to purposefully remember what time and money are really *for*.

In spite of wake-up calls that invite us to consider a slower, more relationship-centered life, there just doesn't seem to have been a nation-wide revival or a shift to a thoughtful pace and enduring values. The American time train still thunders down the tracks, running at the rate of our insatiable love affair with speed. Social commentators call it a "time-crunched culture." Psychologists call it "hurry sickness." Everybody else calls it "multitasking."

This is a familiar topic. Every time we turn around, someone is producing a study on our culture's addiction to hurry and how it is affecting our health, relationships, and general experience of life. Not that we have time to read these reports.

Ours is a 24/7 mindset in which the natural divisions of day and night have been removed, as well as the organic rhythms of seasons that used to give a tempo to human lives. The lights are always on, the drive-through is always open, and the Internet never goes to bed. You can have a cheeseburger at three in the morning, buy a pair of pants from L. L. Bean at dawn, and eat tomatoes in January. (They are pale and as edible as tennis balls, but you can have 'em.)

Don't get me wrong. Except for the tennis-ball tomatoes, this 24/7/365 availability can be a great gift. Believe me, all of us *want* the lights on all the time at emergency rooms across the country. People who work the night shift need access to hot food at 3:00 a.m. Insomniacs everywhere are grateful for what we can get done online in the wee hours.

But if we aren't careful, this luxury of constant access can diminish our attention spans and strip away the virtue of patience.

For example, many of us become aggrieved and offended by the notion of waiting for anything. City life is measured by the "honko-second," the measure of time between the traffic light turning green and the driver of the car behind you blowing his horn. Grown adults stand in front of the elevator anxiously pushing the up button over and over and over, or punch "walk" buttons on traffic signals as if any delay spells doom. We fume at the seconds it takes our computers to access the website we want or roil with road rage at the tollbooth because we chose the line where the driver in front of us dropped his quarter. We punch the buttons on the microwave, tapping our feet with impatience, yell at the child who can't tie his shoe, seethe at the pastor who preaches too long. Chronic impatience becomes bottled wrath.

A typical modern quoted in James Gleick's book, *Faster*, sums up many people's experience. "It has gotten to the point where my days, crammed with all sorts of activities, feel like an Olympic endurance event: the everdayathon.... I hear an invisible stopwatch ticking even when I'm supposed to be having fun."[3]

The use of amphetamines — popularly known, of course, as "speed" — has jumped in the American workplace by 70 percent since 1998. Workers use various illegal forms of the drug in order to boost productivity, energy, and their cadence in the workplace. Those who go faster get more done, supposedly. Those who get more done are promoted. Those who are promoted have more to do in less time and need more, uh, speed. In the end, this kind of acceleration-driven lifestyle, whether in the frenzy of Wall Street or any lesser-known street's office, school, or home — leads to a nervous, shallow experience of life that is lived always in the future.

"When I get promoted, then I'll slow down." "When the kids are all in school ...," "when I graduate ...," "when I make partner ...," "when I retire ..." It boils down to "when-then" thinking: the notion that "when I get to point X in my future, then I will relax and enjoy my life."

The problem with this when-then Zen is that "then" never arrives, and suddenly, it's all over — perhaps in the startling day of smoky catastrophe or in the perplexing final hour in the retirement home, the nursing home, or the hospital. Time runs out, and life was spent hurtling toward some always-elusive future moment that now is gone forever.

If adrenaline flows in response to a chronic state of stress — rather than being on reserve for emergencies — it's like revving a car engine to a hundred miles per hour, then leaving it to idle at that speed.

Adrenaline increases blood cholesterol, narrows the blood vessels, increasing the blood's clotting tendency, and decreases the body's ability to remove cholesterol. Unsurprisingly, this kind of stress is a key factor in heart disease.

It's psychologically damaging as well. We can become addicted to adrenaline, like just about anything else except tofu, and go through withdrawal if we don't have the rush of its arousal. Hence the craving for speed, chaos, overwork. Speed itself feeds a thrill ... when we go fast, the pleasure-chemicals epinephrine and norepinephrine surge through us.

The 24/7 acceleration mindset not only corrodes the central nervous system and the heart, it expresses itself in what appears to be a national attention-deficit and hyperactivity disorder. People are so jangled and hurried that they can devote attention only in fragmented ways. TV producers consider news stories over three minutes' duration to be "long form," and mix them with quicker fare so we won't change the channel. Many of the "wired generation" of teenagers have attention spans measured in tiny little text bits, their brains a muddled puddle of split-screen soup. And the guy next to you on the highway this morning was talking on his cell phone, shaving, and checking his email, all at about 65 miles per hour.

What about us? Where are we on the "Speed and Impatience" scale used by researchers to assess stressed personalities?[4] Here's a handy test to see if you're about to go over the brink.

- *Concern with clock time*: Compared with others, are you more frequently checking your watch? Are you habitually concerned with what time it is?
- *Speech patterns*: Do you talk faster than others you know? Do people have to ask you to slow down? Do you interrupt when someone takes too long to get to his or her point?
- *Eating habits*: Are you the first person to finish your meal? Do you wolf down your food, or do you enjoy it?

- *Walking speed*: Do others have to ask you to slow down? Do you ever meander?
- *Driving*: Do you become excessively annoyed in slow traffic? Do you habitually drive over the speed limit?
- *Schedules*: Are you addicted to setting schedules? Do you allocate certain amounts of time for certain activities? Is punctuality supremely important to you?
- *List making*: Do you make lists compulsively? Do you make lists of what to do on vacation? Do you make lists of your lists?
- *Nervous energy*: Do you become irritable on holidays, days off, or when "there's nothing to do"?
- *Waiting*: Do you become more annoyed than most people if you have to wait in line? Do you sometimes walk out of restaurants or stores if you encounter even a short wait?
- *Alerts*: Do your friends and family tell you to slow down, to take it easier?

Obviously, we all exhibit some of these tendencies sometimes. But if our usual, day-to-day behavior fits most or all of these categories, then we probably have what is nicely called a "time-urgent personality." When this kind of time urgency becomes extreme, as in an addiction to urgency that controls us internally even when there is no external reason to rush, then we are in cardiac and stress danger. We've caught that modern disease called "hurry sickness."[5]

✎

Speed and time-saving tools are wonderful indeed as they serve *true effectiveness* in our lives and don't obscure what time and life are really for (as we'll explore in the next chapter). But as Carl Honore says in *In Praise of Slowness*, "The problem is that our love of speed, our obsession with doing more and more in less and less time, has gone too far; it *has turned into an addiction, a kind of idolatry.*"[6]

Honore doesn't appear to be writing from a biblical perspective, which makes all the more interesting his reference to idolatry. It is clear that human beings are wired to devote ourselves to something or someone. Whatever captivates us most will crowd out competing interests.

Psalm 115 makes an intriguing point about such idols: "Those who make them will be like them."[7] People become more and more like whatever captivates their attention. People who get hooked on hurry are at first just trying to get more done in less time. Then the addiction clicks in, and they end up devoted to speed for speed's sake. They become just like their idol: *fast*.

And at high speed, anything that takes too much time—like helping the weak, needy, and slow, or cultivating real relationships with family, friends, and God Himself—is thrown behind, left like litter on the sideline of a race to nowhere fast.

CHAPTER 11

Wild Jesus and
the Secret of Time

⁓

*The great merchandise of the Church of God is concerned with things
that belong to the Lord Himself, not with their own things,
not with their own enterprises, not with their own merchandise;
not with their own organizations; but with the goods, the wealth of Jesus,
purchased at infinite cost, and now offered to ... the whole human race.
He has left these goods with His servants while He is away.*

G. Campbell Morgan

It's nothing new to note the twenty-first-century pressure cooker that makes many of us sweat. It is important, though, to reconsider one of the questions with which we started this book. In a culture marked by "hurry sickness," how then do we live? Are we stressed and obsessed by time? Or are we at peace? Is there a distinctive that believers can really employ and enjoy in our relationship with time?

No, we don't wear different watches—you know, nice *Christian* watches, sold only in *Christian* bookstores, set to "*Christian* Standard Time," with little alarms that go off when it's time for church. Nor do believers perceive it in a different way scientifically, as in what time *is*, just as we don't think of oxygen in a different way, chemically, than people who don't choose to believe in Christ.

But believers do perceive oxygen—every breath we take—as a gift. In the same way, time itself is a gift. It's not a right to which we are entitled, something we use however we want. This is where believers differ from those who have chosen no allegiance to the Gift-giver.

73

The biblical distinctive is a mindset called stewardship. Its core presupposition is the fact that the money, stuff, talents, and time that believers have at our disposal are not really ours. They belong to God. We're stewards of *His* assets. He has left them to us for a while to manage. We don't know just how long that while is ... but we are to use everything we've been given for God's eternal purposes, not our temporal ones. Time is the medium, in this life, in which we give glory to God by doing His will.

The rich, ancient notion of stewardship doesn't really strike a chord with many twenty-first century Americans. It is too rooted in cultural norms that are no longer normal: a long-ago gilded world of masters and servants, of stewards managing the holdings of powerful kings. It flies in the face of our autonomous, egalitarian assumption that we own our own stuff, including time. Modern readers of the Scriptures can miss the power of this concept because we're put off by its context.

But as we'll see later, if there really is a spiritual secret for living at peace in time, it's connected to a fresh understanding of stewardship, and a new look at Jesus' familiar stories about managers who are given assets to manage while the master is away.

For those of us who seek adventure and drama, an exploration of stewardship sounds like a dubious place to start. It sounds like one of those nice Christian notions that is as dull as over-boiled broccoli but presumably good for you, or at least the Right Thing to Do.

Though many aspects of organized religion have made Jesus as boring as limp broccoli as well, He is anything but. As Dorothy Sayers put it,

> The people who hanged Christ never, to do them justice, accused him of being a bore—on the contrary, they thought him too dynamic to be safe. It has been left for later generations to muffle up that shattering personality and surround him with an atmosphere of tedium. We have very efficiently pared the claws of the Lion of Judah, certified him "meek and

mild," and recommended him as a fitting household pet for pale curates and pious old ladies.[1]

As those in Narnia often say, "He's not a *tame* Lion."

So how did this wild Jesus talk about stewardship, the secret to peace in time? He didn't give long, dry lectures on the topic. He told stories.

Once upon a time, in a land far, far away, Jesus Christ walked the dusty roads of Galilee. He slept outside, swaddled in His big woven robe, His disciples snoring nearby. He ate figs and bread. No broccoli. He smiled when He smelled fresh breezes off the waters of the Sea of Galilee. He was a real person.

During the last few years of His life on earth, in the third decade of the first millennium, Jesus was usually surrounded by lots of other real people. They were poor, rich, smelly, perfumed, illiterate, educated, friends, and skeptics. He told them stories, simple stories that somehow sifted the listeners. Some heard Christ's parables and caught a glimpse of something wonderful. They smelled something Good. They heard something that struck a chord of truth down deep inside, and they smiled. Others would listen to the very same account and hear no chord at all. The story would just make them mad.

The Messiah told these stories in human time, against the great history — well known to His Jewish listeners — of the covenant God had made with His people. The parables are not nice little fables that can be told by any people at any time. They fit into a whole, true story of creation, fall, redemption, and restoration that takes place in *real time* in God's relationship with real people.

One day Jesus told His listeners the story of a wealthy man who went away on a journey. This man called together his senior servants and entrusted his property to them.

This was a common practice in the ancient near East. Since travel to even relatively near-by destinations could take months, landowners would leave their holdings in the hands of trusted servants or slaves, who were expected to manage and multiply the master's assets while he was away. Without flight schedules, cell phones, emails, or telegrams, the servants would not have a clue just when the master would return.

The word Jesus used for "servant" in this story was *doulos*. This meant more than a butler; the original Greek term is that of a slave. It's the same word the apostle Paul used when he spoke of himself as a bond-servant of Jesus—the actual *property* of Christ. The lifework of the *doulos* is all about the Master.

In the story, the master gave one servant five talents of money, to another two, and another one. These "talents" were units of money. We don't know exactly how much, but it doesn't matter. Each servant was given a particular quantity.

The person given five talents "put his money to work" and gained five more.

The person given two talents did the same and gained two more.

The person given one talent "went off, dug a hole in the ground and hid his master's money."

A long time went by.

We'll stop right there, and pick up Christ's story of the stewards a little later.

Though Jesus' teachings regarding stewardship of course apply to the management of any resource, they pack a double whammy when we talk about time.

We are used to hearing them as they apply to money. Jesus spoke frequently about money; a person's attitude toward material things reflects his or her real heart-attitude toward spiritual things. The same is true regarding time—though for many North Americans, time might be even more precious than money.

Time is the one resource given equally to all of us, every day we live. A billionaire and a homeless person both have twenty-four hours in a day. The President of the United States and a prisoner on death row in Zambia both have twenty-four hours in a day. The pastor of the biggest mega-church in America and the pastor of the smallest underground church in China both have twenty-four hours in a day.

Our lives are, of course, different lengths. But we will all be judged by the same standard, whether we live to the age of 24 or 104: how did we use the time we were given?

We can't stockpile time for "later." It passes, relentlessly.

But by the choices we make, and the priorities we take, we can maximize and exploit each day's opportunities like an investor, figuring out how to best use each moment for the greatest return—not for ourselves, but for the Master's account. It's for His enrichment and glory that we seek to make the right choices about how to use the time we have, right now, "as long as it is called Today" as the author of Hebrews put it.[2]

Jesus often set His stories about stewardship against the backdrop of His second coming. Like His first arrival, it would be a physical appearance in human history, not a spiritualized event in some other dimension, not an allegory, but an actual return.

This return, however, will not be inauspicious like His first arrival, when He snuck into Bethlehem one night and only his parents, some shepherds, a few wise men, and a barn full of animals knew it.

Christ's return will be a cataclysmic, historical event that will eclipse anything the world has ever experienced. No one knows when it will happen, but when it does, every human being will see Him. If, at that moment, there are seven billion people on the planet, seven billion people will fall on their faces. Every knee will bow. And eventually there will be an inescapable call for everyone to give an accounting of how he or she has managed time, money, and everything else that seemed to be ours—but in fact belonged to God.

CHAPTER 12

Pronto!

∽❦∽

No eye has seen,
no ear has heard,
no mind has conceived
what God has prepared for those who love him.

1 CORINTHIANS 2:9

When Jesus told stories about stewards, the good ones were always looking expectantly for the master's return. They were *intentional* about how they lived. They invested the master's money. But even more critically, they managed time according to the *master's* plans and priorities, not their own.

A while ago my buddy Jerry and I were talking about this. We talked about living in a way that builds up Christ's Kingdom and counts for eternity. Jerry had just been to the funeral of a prominent, wealthy businessman. This man had been hugely successful and died impossibly rich. He had also been rather litigious and had sued his ex-wife, his children, and numerous competitors. A trail of fractured relationships littered his road to success.

At the memorial service, the flowers, soon to wilt, were gorgeous. The coffin, soon to be covered with dirt, was the best money could buy. But none of the attendees had anything, really, that they could say about the tycoon's legacy. This man was rich in everything—except in what mattered. He had gained much of his world and lost his soul.

Jerry and I talked about the difference between that memorial service and those we'd attended where the deceased person had invested his or her lifetime for God. Lightly—but also seriously—we agreed that going to funerals is a useful practice. The solemnity of remembering a life well or poorly lived can remind us what is truly important in how we use time.

Ironically, just a week after that talk with Jerry, I did get news of a funeral to attend. Jerry's brother Brad, age forty-seven, was fit, lean, and energetic. And while on a mission trip to Guatemala, in the very act of building an orphanage for poor children, he had a massive heart attack and pitched to the ground. He died instantly.

We could not conceive of the fact that Brad was at one moment pouring concrete in Guatemala and the next in another dimension altogether, looking on the face of Jesus.

Brad's widow, Connie, flew to Guatemala to bring home her husband's body. On the plane, she thought back to the trip they had taken together just a few months earlier. They hadn't taken a vacation for many years, but they had gone to Italy, laughing and exploring the countryside like kids. While there, they had wondered why Italians always answered their cell phones, "*Pronto!*" They could understand if it was *buongiorno*, but what in the world did *pronto* mean?

It's just an expression, a local told them. Literally, it means, "I'm ready!" It's slang to let the one who's calling know you're ready to take his call.

Brad and Connie had talked about it. It's just like the Holy Spirit, they had said. When He calls us to do something, we need to be ready.

Pronto!

Connie smiled as she thought of that wonderful time in Italy. She was so glad to have those great memories, now that Brad was gone.

For his funeral, Brad's Pennsylvania church was full of music, flowers, and friends. At the front was a simple table with a single candle and a photo of Brad with his arm around Connie. His hammer lay there too, and his worn work boots, laces untied. Further back, to the left, was his casket.

Brad was a quiet man, a background person. His pastor told us he would have been quite uncomfortable with his eulogies; he would have snuck out the back door rather than hear the outpouring of acclaim. He wasn't a celebrity.

But Brad was a hero. Person after person testified how he had helped them. No one knew he had been involved in so many areas of need or how much he had come through.

Then it was Connie's turn to speak. She stood at the altar and talked frankly about the tough times she and Brad had weathered. But twelve years earlier, they had made a conscious decision to make Christ the center of how they lived and to make every moment count, as best they could. They had cultivated their marriage. She had quit her corporate position so she could invest more time at home and in the work of their church. Brad had scaled back his own career and made countless trips to places of need, building orphanages, caring for children in crisis, and at one point, giving the shoes right off his feet to a man who'd lost his home—and everything else—in a hurricane. Brad had come home shoeless, and the man had gone on to a new home and a new relationship with Jesus because of Brad.

"I look back," said Connie, weeping yet strong, "and I have no regrets."

No regrets. When you walk in a cemetery, some of the gravestones are ornate, glossy Italian marble with expensive carvings and elaborate flourishes. Some are spare and simple. But all have the same four elements: a name, a birth year, a death year, and a dash between those two dates. It is what we do in that dash that counts. How are we managing the time the Master has given us?

Believers exist in time, of course, and yet simultaneously we live with our hopes staked in eternity. We are like a mountain climber who has thrown his grappling hook and secured his weight in the cleft of the rock high above. We trust our lives and conduct ourselves as we climb, with our security based on what is above, not on what we can see in front of us.

So Brad was able to disengage from what the busy achievers all around him were doing. He decided to slow down his business life and speed up his Christian service. He wouldn't have said anyone else needed to do it just like he had. He just obeyed God's calling for *him*—which makes what Connie found out about Brad's actual moment of death so significant.

That morning Brad had been working on the roof of the Guatemalan orphanage. He was with eight or nine other guys, and they were working with a cement mixer. Brad and his partner, Jared, were taking turns pouring the heavy cement. It was hot, hard work.

It had been Brad's turn pouring cement for a while, and Jared kept asking him if he was tired. "You ready for me to take it, Brad?"

"No, I'm okay," Brad would say.

A few minutes later Jared asked again.

"No, not yet, thanks," Brad said.

Then all of a sudden Brad straightened up. Jared looked over … but Brad wasn't looking at him. He was gazing up, toward something or someone that Jared could not see.

"I'm ready!" Brad said. And then he dropped his tools and fell to the ground, dead.

He had gotten the call.

Pronto!

CHAPTER 13

Extremes:
The Sloth and the Controller

Tell me what you think of time,
and I shall know what to think of you.
J. T. FRASER,
FOUNDER OF THE INTERNATIONAL SOCIETY
FOR THE STUDY OF TIME[1]

Brad was wise in his use of time. When I look back at portions of my own life, I swung between two equally unhealthy extremes about time and its use. One looked lazy, and it was. That was when I was a Sloth. The other may have looked productive, but it wasn't. That's when I was a Controller.

I inadvertently became a Sloth during college. A godly older woman came to our dorm each Thursday evening for a Bible study. The idea was that she would mentor my roommates and me. For my part, I hoped I would grow up to be as disciplined and attractive as she was.

One exercise I remember was that our leader gave us calendar sheets with each day broken into half-hour increments. In an effort to become more mindful of our time usage, we were to fill them out with our daily course schedules and then shade in different colors on the blocks for different types of activities. Red for classes, green for studying, blue for meals, purple for exercise, gray for sleeping, gold for devotional times, pink for time blocks in which we would write letters home with our quill pens since this was before the Internet existed.

I neatly filled out my calendar, full of high hopes, humming lightly and shading the different sections in bright colors. My week looked like a pleasing patchwork quilt. I loved the notion of life proceeding along in such an orderly way, the minutes marching by like soldiers, the contents of my hours on a conveyor belt, everything under control. I knew that if I did all these things, I would emerge from college a lovely woman of God.

I posted my calendar above my desk ... and then sadly, disastrously, slothfully ignored it for four years.

I don't know why I didn't follow through on the execution of those good disciplines. Perhaps I was worn out from all that coloring. Perhaps my faith was in my brain only, its truths like files in my mental software, but it hadn't been installed on the hard drive of my heart. It didn't run my defaults.

At any rate, there was little relation between my use of time and the Christianity that I alleged to believe. I ignored commitments, skipped class, snubbed exercise, overindulged in the dining hall, particularly on Assorted Pie Night, and, with a hard heart and a soft head, attended way too many fraternity parties. I squandered many of those 2,903,040 multicolored half-hour blocks of my college days. This total does not include summer vacations. I was a terrible steward of the time God had loaned me. By the springtime of my senior year, I could be found lounging on a striped beach towel in the sunny quad, listening to Boz Scaggs and snoozing like a walrus at the zoo.

I woke up in time for graduation.

During graduate school, my walrus ways began to change, and eventually I swung to the other extreme and became a Controller with a super-busy pseudo-steward mindset.

My transition to this high-pitched state was in part because my first job out of graduate school (aside from waitressing in a busy French restaurant, which had its own time pressures like the need to speedily deliver flaming desserts to patrons' tables without setting my hair on fire in the process) was with Chuck Colson, a man who mastered multitasking before the term was invented. Chuck was then—as now—an enormously productive triple-A personality who scribbled article outlines on dinner napkins, dictated brilliant book memoranda in taxis, and made detailed backup plans to foil any contingencies, be they rain, snow, sleet, hail, airline strikes, or major surgery. Nothing would stop him from his appointed duties.

In my youthful fervor, I adopted this super-productive mindset without the underlying spiritual maturity that should inform it.

In the midst of writing multiple projects on tight deadlines, I began to make lists of my lists. I worked feverishly on trains, planes, and automobiles. Had I but paper enough, and pens, I felt I could control the course of the next twenty-four hours down to the minute. I wasn't coloring them in different pastels—no time for that—but I was pretty manic about trying to get the biggest bang for my time-buck.

As the years went by, through my twenties and into my thirties, fun factors were added. One husband. Three children. A wooly, mammoth dog. The equations got more complicated. Houses, moves, committees, carpools. My life was then—as now—a tangle of schedules, commitments, calendars. My life verse, then, was from Job: "My days are swifter than a weaver's shuttle," and I felt like it was a space shuttle, zipping back and forth in a giant loom, madly weaving the threads of my days. I could not see a pattern; I was just zooming the loom, dizzy and seeing stars.

During this period I didn't think much about stewardship, really. I would have agreed intellectually that yes, yes, of course, everything belonged to God—time, treasure, talents—and I was simply a manager of the resources He had given me.

But in reality, I was not practicing real biblical *stewardship* because I had unconsciously replaced it with a false god of "time management."

My notion of "redeeming the time" mostly had to do with measurable productivity, that swift-running conveyor belt full of things, events, products, and papers. I knew a lot about my own determined efforts—workworkwork—but I knew little about God's supernatural power and *His* timing. It was as if I took a spiritual principle and then tried to execute it solely through earthly means. The result was a constant sense of uneasy confusion; I was rarely at peace in time because I usually felt like I should be doing something else.

For example, if I was working on a weekend I felt guilty, like I should be taking a walk or learning to knit or making thumbprint cookies with the children, like all good mothers do. Of course, if I was doing any of those things—not that I will ever knit—then I felt guilty because I wasn't doing something that was vocationally "productive."

Should someone with a need ring my doorbell unexpectedly, I'd want to hide—in spite of the fact that my belief system told me people were more important than schedules. My skewed and anxious attitude about time affected my ability to act on principles I really believed.

Now, as you realize, the depictions in these pages aren't entirely accurate: I've caricatured both of them, painting with a broad brush both my post-graduate nervous-driven life and my walrus days at the university. They weren't all bad.

But this broad point is worth sharpening. I spent way too long with an unhealthy attitude regarding time. When I was a Sloth I knew little of real rest. When I was a Controller, I knew little of lasting productivity.

I don't know what your story is regarding time. Everyone has a different tempo; we all speed up or slow down in different seasons of our lives. But as I've talked with friends and interviewed acquaintances, I've seen that the two extremes I described are not unique to me. They mirror the ways that many people live, so it's useful to consider them more carefully. It's intriguing too—because though the sofa-lolling, time-wasting Sloth and the multitasking, time-obsessed Controller may look very different on the outside, they share similar characteristics on the inside.

CHAPTER 14

Slug Time:
The Long and Slimy Trail

*Eternity is a terrible thought.
I mean, where's it all going to end?*
TOM STOPPARD

Sloth is an archaic concept. You just don't hear much about it anymore. Literally, it comes from the Middle English *slouthe*, or slow, and refers to any of the slow-moving arboreal edentate mammals that comprise two genera (*Bradypus* and *Choloepus*), inhabit tropical forests of South and Central America, hang from the branches back downward, and feed on fruits, shoots, and leaves.

This definition is not the one with which we are going to concern ourselves.

According to Webster, sloth also refers to laziness or spiritual apathy as in "the deadly sin of sloth." Modern people aren't as familiar with the seven deadly sins as were the citizens of the Middle Ages, who lived in mortal fear of their funky punishments in hell. The official list came from monastic theologians who identified a core set of offenses that shared, on an increasing scale, a preoccupation with self rather than with God. They were lust, gluttony, covetousness, sloth, anger, envy, and pride.

These evils aren't much a part of our national conversation today, except as they're used, with a glossy spin, to market everything from beer to luxury cars. They also surface in esoteric Internet discussions about how each of the deadlies is represented by a character on

"Gilligan's Island," that classic TV show from the 1960s (which is not quite the Middle Ages, but close).

Students of the show advance the theory that the Professor exhibits the deadly sin of pride: anyone who can make a radio out of two coconuts and some wire must regard himself way too highly. Ginger, the lascivious movie star, represents lust. Envy goes to Maryann, who wanted to be Ginger. Thurston Howell the Third, who took a large trunk full of money on a three-hour cruise, is greed. Since Mrs. Howell never did much of anything at all, she is sloth.

At this point the analysts run into a problem. We are left with the sins of anger and gluttony, and the mad and corpulent Skipper personifies them both. This leaves only Gilligan. But Gilligan, in fact, was the *reason* that the other characters got trapped on their island of despair in the first place. He was also the means by which their hopes of escape were foiled, week after week. He therefore represents the Devil.

But let us return to the specific sin of sloth.

Most of us don't know many people, aside from teenagers, whom we would characterize as sloths. Most respectable grownups are known, after all, for their diligent activity and deep-rooted work ethic. Not too many of us are lying around doing nothing.

But this is worth a deeper look, because the sin of sloth can invade even the busiest life. In fact, it tends to infect lives that are too busy, full of too many things. Though we tend to lump sloth with laziness, it isn't necessarily physical idleness.[1] It's more of an attitude, a *spiritual* idleness. The Latin term for it was *acedia*, which means "not caring." Slothful people might well run around doing everything or lie around doing nothing. The core problem, either way, is that they *feel* nothing. Down deep, they don't care.

As Dorothy Sayers has said,

In the world it is called Tolerance, but in hell it is called Despair. It is the sin that believes in nothing, cares for nothing, seeks to know nothing, interferes with nothing, enjoys noth-

ing, hates nothing, finds purpose in nothing, lives for nothing, and remains alive because there is nothing for which it
will die.[2]

At its root, sloth doesn't care enough about anything—God,
neighbors, or even self—for its soul to be truly stirred. It's a weary
indifference toward God and His gifts.

This hollowness is different from depression caused by chemical
imbalance, stress, or tragedy. Sloth is not illness, fatigue, or sorrow.
It is soul apathy that feels, down deep, that nothing that I do will *really* make a difference in the end. Sloth can be expressed both as do-
nothingness—or extreme busyness that covers up the apathy within
so the person doesn't have to face its core cause.

Frederick Buechner writes that the sloth is a person

> who goes through the motions, who flies on automatic pilot.
> Like a man with a bad head cold, he has mostly lost his sense
> of taste and smell. He knows something is wrong with him,
> but not wrong enough to do anything about. Other people
> come and go, but through glazed eyes he hardly notices them.
> He is letting things run their course. He is getting through
> his life.[3]

Going through the motions is not all bad. There are days where
we have to do what we don't feel like doing, tending the child or
leading the meeting or cleaning up the mess, even though we have
no grand passion to do so. But there is a perennial *negativity* to those
who are slothful, whether they are active or idle. In effect, they
are running the clock out, tolerating their days, getting by, killing
time.

This is why sloth—whether expressed in do-nothing hours
slumped in front of the television or in soulless activity—is so
deadly. By means of it the enemy of our souls chills us to the core
and causes us to perceive the precious time we're given as a tedious
burden rather than a gift.

As C. S. Lewis's Screwtape wrote to his fellow devil,

The Christians describe [God] as one "without whom Nothing is strong." And Nothing is very strong: strong enough to steal away a man's years not in sweet sins but in a dreary flickering of the mind over it knows not what and knows not why, in the gratification of curiosities so feeble that the man is only half aware of them, in drumming of fingers and kicking of heels, in whistling tunes that he does not like, or in the long, dim labyrinth of reveries that have not even lust or ambition to give them a relish, but which, once chance association has started them, the creature is too weak and fuddled to shake off.[4]

The Bible talks more about slugs than sloths, but they are cut from the same slimy cloth. Portions of the ancient book of Proverbs nail the unfulfilled, anxious, selfish character of the sloth in a way that any modern reader can relate.

Some years ago the *Chicago Tribune* published a series of articles on the Seven Deadly Sins. The commentaries were secular in tone, but their observations about sloth sound similar to Proverbs.

Sloth is insidious. It whispers that you might as well do it tomorrow, that nobody will know if you cut corners here and there to save yourself some trouble, that the world will be the same in a hundred years no matter what you do, so why do anything? ...

Sloth hits the snooze alarm, hits the remote control, and hits the road when the going gets tough ... Sloth cheats on exams, drinks straight from the milk carton and leaves exactly two sheets on the toilet roll so that it will have to be replaced by the next poor soul.... Sloth has never written a thank-you note, sent a birthday card on time or entertained angels. All of this simply takes too much effort.[5]

This description reminds me of what doctors say about people with "passive-aggressive personalities." They might seem to comply with the desires and needs of others, but actually resist them, at the same time becoming increasingly hostile and angry. Therapists identify this syndrome by the following symptoms:

> procrastination
> intentional inefficiency
> avoiding responsibility
> complaining
> blaming others
> resentment
> sullenness
> resistance to suggestions from others
> unexpressed anger or hostility
> fear of authority

If we keep this list in mind, as well as the slimy character of the sluggy sloth, they both bring fresh insight to Jesus' story about the stewards and the talents. Where were we?

CHAPTER 15

Steward Little

In the midst of a world of light and love,
of song and feast and dance,
[Lucifer] could find nothing to think of
more interesting than his own prestige.
C. S. Lewis, *A Preface to Paradise Lost*

May the knowledge of Thy eternity
not be wasted on me!
A. W. Tozer

Ah, yes. Two of the stewards had invested the master's assets that were entrusted to them. The third had buried his. And the master was away.

What did the servants do during those months or years of the master's absence? They went about their usual schedules. They worked, ate, slept, dreamed. Presumably, the ones who put the master's money to work looked forward to his return, consciences clear. They were on the lookout for fresh investment opportunities and grinned when the master's holdings multiplied.

Since the third servant didn't have an investment to manage, maybe he never thought about it. Maybe, in slothlike fashion, he felt as though nothing he did would make a difference anyway, so he did nothing. Maybe he felt nothing.

Or perhaps the slothful steward was *consumed* by that hidden talent. It was out of sight but not out of mind. Maybe he obsessively worried that he really should be doing something with it. Perhaps he lived in fear that thieves would find it. Maybe he minded his hole, hiding in a nearby bush wearing a branch on his head, watching what might happen. After all, when the master returned, he was able to recover the talent, so it's not like he had forgotten where it was. Maybe it was constantly on his mind, a heavy burden, a dull pain.

At any rate, when the master finally returned, it was time to settle accounts. The first and second servants had both doubled the master's investment. Whether one is given a little or a lot, what matters is how a person manages what he or she is given—so both were commended equally, with identical language: "Well done, good and faithful servant! You have been faithful with a few things; I will put you in charge of many things." Then came the invitation to riches far greater: "Come and share your master's happiness!" or, as some translations read, "Enter into the master's *joy!*"

Then Mr. Hole Digger was called forward. He had the master's talent with him, clods of dirt still sticking to it. "Master," he began. He knew who was in charge. On the day of accounting, even this conflicted individual had no illusions about to whom the talent *really* belonged.

But then the servant got it all wrong. "I knew that you are a hard man, harvesting where you have not sown and gathering where you have not scattered seed. So I was afraid and went out and hid your talent in the ground."

One imagines those sad words just hanging in the air for a moment. As G. Campbell Morgan puts it, the third servant had a false mental picture of the master. Then "the lord refuted that lie by repeating it to him. One cannot read the words without catching the note of irony, of satire.... 'Is that what you know, that I reaped where I did not sow, and gather where I did not scatter? Is that your estimate? Well, if you think that way, you might have put my money to the bankers, and at least I should have had interest on my return!' "[1]

As Morgan says, the third servant's huge error was that he didn't discern the master's character. Though he gave him lip service, he envisioned the master as far too small. He turned him into a creation of his own dim imagination, a convenience to justify his own behavior.

To use a modern catch-phrase, he also seemed to be living in denial that his master would ever really return. After all, it was comfortable on the master's estate. All his needs were met, and more. Day after day, the sun rose and set, and the master didn't return. Life as usual. Whatever.

The servant had plenty of time to wake up and smell the coffee. He could have profited from the example of the other servants who really understood the nature of the master, the reality of his return, and how to make time work for them. He could have repented, gotten out his shovel, dug up that buried talent, and invested it.

But no: to return to our list of classic passive-aggressive tendencies, the slothful steward exhibited them all. He procrastinated. He was intentionally inefficient. He avoided responsibility. He complained. He blamed others—in fact, he brazenly blamed the master himself—"it's not my fault, it's *your* fault since you're such a tough boss!"

He showed resentment and sullenness, simmering anger, and we can infer he resisted suggestions from others, since he had plenty of time to follow the examples of the good stewards but didn't. Lastly, he demonstrated fear of authority. Ironically, it wasn't holy fear of God, which is a good thing, but misinformed anxiety about just whom he was dealing with.

This is the deadly error of the sloth. Whether he is extremely busy or lying all day on a Barcalounger, when it comes to time, the sloth wastes or resents it and resists the master's authority—because he doesn't acknowledge, in the depths of his heart, just who the master really is.

How does this apply in my life? In yours?

Again, though the story is about managing money, it applies to any resource God gives us to handle, set against the timeline backdrop of the Master's return.

Being a good steward of time doesn't start with managing it better. It doesn't begin with being more organized, efficient, and

disciplined. These are great virtues. But one can be the most organized person on the planet and still have a heart as cold as steel,
locked tight as a heavy file cabinet, a heart that does not really acknowledge the master's rights to all those files.

A number of years ago I heard a real-life modern variation of
the steward story. The steward in question worked with an international ministry that had local offices in various countries, with
its administrative headquarters in the U.S. The man had been given
management of part of a large, unnamed continent. All right, I'll tell
you: it was Africa.

For months the manager's boss had contacted him repeatedly,
asking for a certain set of files and donation records. These held key
information about the work in Africa and how the manager had
enhanced it since the boss's last visit. The manager promised to send
the files, over and over. There was always some fresh excuse. But
they never arrived.

One day the boss got on a plane. He got off in Africa, hired
a driver, and made his way to the slothful manager's office. Un-
announced, he entered and cheerfully asked for the files.

Once the employee had been revived from his faint, he claimed
that the key to the file cabinet had been stolen. "Stolen, I tell you!"

"Oh?" said the boss. He went out to a nearby construction site
and politely borrowed a pick-axe and other tools. When he came
back, he asked the errant manager to step aside, and he hacked open
the cabinet.

As you can imagine, the files were not there. Perhaps they were
buried in a field somewhere. The bad manager had squandered the
boss's resources. And he had lied to himself and others so much that
he no longer even knew what the truth was. He did not believe that
the boss would ever come so far and ask him, face to face, for an
accounting.

Perhaps we're not as shady or blatant as that manager in Africa.
But do we believe, really, that Christ will come so far and ask us for
an accounting of how we have used His time?

CHAPTER 16

Mission: Control!

Time is more important than money.
Time measures the pace of your life.
Money provides the means.
Effective people attain more money by mastering time....
If you want to advance . . .
if you desire success . . . you must master time.
SALEEM RANA, THE EMPOWERED SOUL

A man is a slave to whatever has mastered him.
2 PETER 2:19

The ways of the Sloth are not hard to identify as a poor approach to time.

But when we go to the other end of the time-usage spectrum as I've laid it out and consider the Controller, his or her methodology can *seem* quite positive. Controllers can appear to be disciplined, productive, and virtuous. They often head committees. They multitask. They know how to manage their minutes to get more done than anyone else.

But if people are control-driven, rather than Spirit-driven, they aren't much fun to be around. They value results more than relationships. They're obsessed with measurable productivity and demonstrate a rigid lack of flexibility that makes it hard for them to respond with grace to unplanned events. They simmer with perpetual negativity and frustration that sometimes erupts into scalding rage.

At the heart, the obsessive, busy, productive time controller demonstrates a central error that is as deadly as the sin of the sloth. In terms of the stewardship parable, the empty sloth doesn't know the nature of the master and doesn't live as though he'll really return. Meanwhile, full of fine intentions, working hard, the time-controller might start as a steward but eventually gets mixed up and thinks he or she *is* the master.

For example, let's move from the stewards' parable to the biblical story of Martha of Bethany. This was not a parable but a real event that took place in real time, when Martha and her siblings Mary and Lazarus hosted Jesus and His friends for a dinner party. Before the meal, Mary sat at Jesus' feet and listened to Him talk. Controller Martha ran around attending to the huge task of getting the meal ready and got upset about it.

Many of us identify more with Martha and secretly detest Mary as useless, though of course we would never say that because it would be unspiritual.

The great thing about these biblical people is that they aren't caricatures. They sometimes get presented that way ... as in Mary the spiritual goody two shoes and Martha the PMS-crazed hostess with the mostest who blew up and had the misfortune of having her tirade recorded in Scripture for, like, eternity. But they were real people with distinct personalities, people with whom we can relate, people whom Jesus loved.

This was an unconventional family. Martha, the eldest, owned the home where Jesus stayed. She was evidently a widow of some economic and social standing in the community. Then we have Mary, who was crazy about Jesus and had unusual insights into who He was and how long He would be with them. Then we have brother Lazarus, whose chief distinction in Scripture is that he was dead and decomposing for a while and then Jesus brought him back to life and put him back together.

About these three the Bible says, simply, "Jesus loved Martha and her sister and Lazarus." He loved them in spite of their inadequacies, which in Lazarus's case included being dead.

Martha's name meant literally "lord" or "master," and this was part of her personality. She was an efficient, competent woman who was used to being in charge. She entertained Jesus not only on this occasion but at the home of Simon the Leper when a feast was given in Jesus' honor, and the Gospels note that Martha served as hostess.[1] Middle Eastern hospitality was lavish; guests usually stayed for at least three days, and hospitality was considered a sacred duty. Food preparation would have taken many hours for even the simplest of meals.

Jesus came to town. He came to Martha's house, which was likely several rooms, two stories, built around a courtyard. The courtyard was used for entertaining guests; Jesus would have been there, perhaps crunching on olives and talking with those who had crowded in to hear him. As we've noted, Mary sat at His feet. Meanwhile, Martha "was distracted by all the preparations that had to be made."

Most of us can relate to that. Even in our day of microwaves, pressure cookers, and every other time-saving device, meals just don't cook themselves. Let alone in a day when dinner was strutting around the barnyard until its number was up. So there were many, many "preparations that had to be made."

We can imagine Martha, supervising servants, wringing necks, running back and forth between water jugs and boiling stewpots, sweating, and getting more and more angry with each passing moment. Her mission? Control!

She'd peek around the corner to the courtyard, where Jesus was, and get madder still. There was that oblivious Mary, lounging around soaking up His every word. There was Lazarus, alive for once, just sitting there. Useless, as usual.

We don't know how long Martha fumed. All we know is that at some point, her pot boiled over. She blew into the courtyard. "Lord!" she cried, seething, red-faced. "Don't you care that my sister has left me to do the work by myself? Tell her to help me!"

Martha had issues. She was furious with Mary. She was trying to use Jesus to reprimand her lazy Twinkie of a sister who would not yield to her control. And though Martha gave lip service to Jesus, calling him "Lord," she had totally lost perspective. True to her name, she was thinking of *herself* as master. She addressed Jesus in a familiar colloquial term as an equal or inferior, demanding His intervention as her right.

Martha had started with the right goal. She wanted to serve Jesus. But she lost sight of how to do that. She turned the objective into making the meal rather than pleasing the Master. Barreling toward her own outcome, she got frustrated by how much there was to be done in so little time. In the process, she forgot who Jesus was, yelling at Him and treating Him like a means to *her* end.

It's so easy to be like Martha, particularly in today's high-achieving culture. Even when we want to serve Jesus, we can end up blown off track, distracted by the means rather than keeping the end goal before us.

Martha was very efficient, no doubt. She was getting a lot done. But there is a difference between efficiency and effectiveness for the Kingdom. Some of us can get hung up with getting so much done that we forget to pull back and assess just *why* we're doing what we're doing. Sometimes we can draw our plans from the world's values rather than God's priorities.

This is unconscious, of course. But sometimes supposedly Christian stewardship is just a religious overlay on secular time management principles.

Well-meaning book jackets tell believers things like "you can get control of your life!" But is more control the answer? It actually feels like part of the problem. As an old friend who is the senior pastor of a large, influential church in another state told me, "I get into a mindset where nothing is safe unless I can control it. By trying to fix many things and control many things, I find that I use many words. But I need to learn to listen. I need to listen to God, and I need to listen to others." (My friend is assisted in this good quest by his wife, who posted a subtle sign in their bathroom: "Please resign as general manager of the universe.")

Meanwhile some preachers extol a mindset that is like a prosperity gospel, except it has to do with time. Prosperity theology says that God blesses His people with material wealth if they have enough faith to receive it. The time-control gospel preaches that our lives will run on schedule and we will be spiritually productive if we just exercise enough discipline, if we just try hard enough and get control of our time. As such, it smells far more of works than grace.

All we need do is purchase the right calendar or software or institute the right system ... if we can just make meals for thirty days and freeze them all to save time later, we'll get ahead of the rat race ... and we will be good stewards. "Make Time for Success!" the glossy brochures tell us. You just need to master the "thirty-nine essential skills needed to take full control of your life!"[2]

Of course, it is great to be organized. But if I'm preoccupied with the mastery of thirty-nine skills, I don't have time to listen for the voice of the Master. It's like a competition in which a dancer focuses so much on the steps—on technical prowess—that she misses the meaning of the dance. The judges will send her away—even if she is mechanically "perfect"—in favor of one whose very soul is connected to the passion of the dance itself.

Please hear what I am saying. Organizational steps, aids, and systems are tremendous tools. But the point here is that "getting control" of time management methods is not all we need to do to be good stewards of time. "Time-saving" skills and devices can help us get more done in fewer minutes—but that's not necessarily the goal. The steward's goal is to serve Christ, to use the time He has given us to extend *His* Kingdom. This means being disciplined, organized, on top of our daily planner—but ready at any moment to deviate from it if the Holy Spirit so leads. It is about trusting God, listening for His voice, and following *His* cues rather than compulsively keeping our own schedules.

If we don't see the big picture of who God is and what time is for, then organizational means will become ends in themselves, and we will become obsessive and harried every time something slips out of our control. Just like Martha. Time management tools are great, but if we look to them in the hope they'll help us "get control" of our lives then we have the wrong goal.

Really, theologically speaking, the journey of the believer is one of *relinquishing* control, not getting more of it. It's a growing understanding and practice of the mindset that our lives are not our own, that everything we have, including time, belongs to the Master.

Perhaps this seems like just semantics. But words often reveal underlying attitudes. I'm reminded of the time I met a man who was part of the worship team for a megachurch that included attendees with deep pockets and shallow theology. I couldn't help but feel that he and some of his colleagues seemed rather full of themselves.

At one point someone asked him what time the church's Saturday evening service started.

"Oh, I perform at seven o'clock," the man began, and then he caught himself and started over: "I mean, we lead worship at seven."

His first choice of words seemed to show his heart. His view of his role seemed to have a lot more to do with "performing" for others rather than reverencing God.

In the same way, it's easy to nod to stewardship but still speak of "my" time and "my" plans and "my" life.

Granted, we don't want to sound sanctimonious, speaking piously of "God's time" as we glance at the clock. But words can reveal our real view regarding ownership.

Jesus told the story of a certain rich man who had an incredible year. His holdings grew so much that he had no place to store them all, and there was no "Hold Everything" catalogue by which he could send away for more storage.

"What shall I do?" he thought.

Then it came to him. *I'll tear down my barns and build bigger ones! Then I can store all my stuff. I'll have plenty of good things laid up for years to come. Bring out the margaritas and the karaoke machine ... "take life easy; eat, drink and be merry!"*[3]

Then, said Jesus, God invades the timeline.

"But God said to him, 'You fool! This very night your life will be demanded from you. Then who will get what you have prepared for yourself?'"

This person—this fool, as God called him—was restless in the quest for continual, conspicuous consumption. Everything, he thought, was his: *my* crops, *my* barns, *my* grain, *my* goods ... *MY* life.

The problem though, was that his presupposition was incorrect. It wasn't all his. It was on loan and could be demanded from him by the true Owner at any point in time.

Today, as in Jesus' day, it's so easy to adopt that kind of thinking. *Mine, mine, mine.* We wouldn't do it consciously, but it's so easy to think just like the world but to gild secular thinking with a shiny spiritual gold-leaf veneer of "Christian" language.

So, regarding our view of time, we might call it "stewardship," but maybe it's just a religious version of the world's "time management." And the world around us, just like in Jesus' day, runs after many things. As we noted earlier, the modern American pace is so often driven by the clock, not from priorities within. The cultural drumbeat can drown out what is most important: snared by the jungle rhythm, we make our sacrifices at the altar of time, going faster, faster, faster, in order to be highly effective, productive, and efficient.

In his hit book *The Tipping Point*, Malcolm Gladwell cites a Princeton University study that shows how people's preoccupation with time can create an often-oblivious disconnect between what they believe and how they behave.

Two psychologists met with a group of seminarians from Princeton Seminary. They asked each one to prepare an address on a given biblical theme—like the parable of the Good Samaritan—then to walk to a nearby building to present it to an audience. On the way to their presentation, each student encountered a man slumped in an alley, moaning in pain, evidently the victim of a street crime. As you can guess, the psychologists wanted to see which of the seminary students would be a real-life Good Samaritan to this man who looked like he was in dire need.

The psychologists introduced several variables into the experiment. First, they gave the participants a questionnaire that included questions about why they had decided to study theology. Did they see it as a means for personal spiritual fulfillment? Or were they looking to serve others? The researchers also varied the topics for the students' presentations. The final factor was this: as the experimenter would send the student over to the building where the speech was to take place, he would look at his watch and say, "Oh, you're late. They were expecting you a few minutes ago. Better get moving!"

To other students he would say, "It'll be a few minutes before they're ready for you, but you might as well head over now."

What happened when the students encountered the seemingly injured man in the alley?

Some stopped and helped; some didn't. Oddly enough, the variables we assume might make a difference did not. We would think that those who had reported they were entering the ministry in order to help people would aid the hurt man ... or surely, those who were on their way to give a talk about the Good Samaritan would help!

But those factors didn't make any predictable difference. Some people aided the man; some didn't. Amazingly, the psychologists reported, "On several occasions a seminary student going to give his talk on the parable of the Good Samaritan literally stepped over the victim as he hurried on his way" to the lecture hall.

The *only* factor that dependably made a foreseeable difference in the seminarians' behavior was if they were in a hurry or not. Of the participants who were told they were running late, only 10 percent helped the ailing man. Of the students who were told they had time to spare, 63 percent stopped to help.

Malcolm Gladwell concludes that

> what this study is suggesting ... is that the convictions of your
> heart and the actual contents of your thoughts are less impor-
> tant ... in guiding your actions than the immediate context

of your behavior. The words, "Oh, you're late," had the effect of making someone who was ordinarily compassionate into someone who was indifferent to suffering.

Gladwell says that seemingly small environmental factors can shape behavior. Time's perceived scarcity or plenty can spur people to do things—or not do things—more so than the beliefs they *say* are most important.

This was just an experiment, of course. But it makes me wonder. How many times do we step over a wounded neighbor—figuratively speaking—because we're in a hurry? How often do we yell at Jesus because other people aren't doing their part and time is running out? Are we living—in real time—at odds with what we say are our most deeply held beliefs? At root, are we often like Martha, distracted and controlling, acting like it's *our* time, not God's?

CHAPTER 17

How Big Is Your God?

ॐ

Our souls yearn for a wonder that reaches beyond the dimensions
of our finite minds, and if we don't allow a wonder toward God,
we'll search for it elsewhere, in false gods. . . .
The older you get, the more it takes to fill your heart with wonder. . .
and only God is big enough to do that.

RAVI ZACHARIAS

Freedom from the "whatever" mindset of the Slothful Steward or the "I am master" manacle of the Mission Controller requires the same key. Wherever we might find ourselves on the gamut between sloth and control, if we want real peace and purpose in our relationship with time in this harried world, we need to reset our "life as usual" perspectives. In the end, if we want to "come and enter into the joy of the master" (which we'll discuss in Part Four), the secret to doing so is seeing life and time according to the Master's point of view, not our own.

We alluded to this earlier when we spoke of a few little things like God and eternity in chapter 8. Now we get to unpack this case.

What comes into your mind when you think about God?

Your answer will give a good idea of what your life is really like today, and where you are headed tomorrow. "We tend, by a secret law of the soul, to move toward our mental image of God," A. W. Tozer wrote.[1] It is incredibly important that our idea of God correspond as nearly as possible to the true being of God. We may not even be aware of our real idea of God; it may well be buried under nice religious window dressing.[2]

What *is* our unvarnished perception of God? What are our private prayers like, away from the proper pious phrases that come so readily to some of us during group prayers? How do we think about God in the car, in the office, in the school, in the home ... or do entire days go by with God mounted on the back wall of our brain like a "break glass in case of emergency" case that is under *our* sovereign control? Is our conception of God really just a gilded, extended edition of our own wishes, ideas, and desires?

Certainly, in our limited human condition, we cannot think of God as He really is. But if we are drawing our image of God from the wrong sources, then our God is too small. God can't be found in unsanctified imaginations or in the caricatures of pop culture. He is not The Man Upstairs. He does not "help those who help themselves." God is not the proud grandpa of a bouncing bloodline of Merovian kings. He is not our copilot.

And He's not you or me, no matter how many spiritual guides say things like this: "It is time for you to accept that the God within is your higher self.... Understand that when you say God, you refer to your higher self."[3]

God has not left us clueless as to His identity. Though human beings cannot know God in His fullness, the royal treasury of His attributes is available to those who humbly hunt for Him. The only way to learn what God is really like is to pursue His revealed clues: His creation, His Word, and His Son.[4]

Regarding creation, the apostle Paul said that human beings have ample means to perceive God's characteristics through the natural world around us. But some choose to ignore Him rather than glorify Him and give thanks to Him. As a result, they become easy marks for idol worship of all kinds.

Some do so in obvious ways, exchanging, "the glory of the immortal God for images made to look like mortal man and birds and animals and reptiles."[5]

When I was in a rural part of northeastern India a while ago, I traveled through a village during a feast to a Hindu goddess of wisdom. Every corner had a brightly colored tent erected in her honor. We passed small trucks that were transporting plastic images of the goddess to be delivered to the worship tents. In the open backs of the pickups were tangled heaps of goddess manikins, arms and legs sticking stiffly every which way like rigid roadkill. Once delivered, they were set up so local people could enter the tents, bow reverently, and leave offerings of money and fruit in exchange for a blessing of wisdom from the plastic goddess.

In another part of the country, I visited villages where people worshiped sacred trees, circling and touching them in daily rituals of worship so their lives would run well.

These are the types of mental pictures that occur to most of us when we think about idolatry. As a result, many modern readers skip over portions of Romans 1 because the references to idol worship just don't seem relevant.

But there is plenty here to engage urbane twenty-first-century people—particularly as we consider what this notion of the bigness of God has to do with our core topic of time.

Tozer says that the essence of idolatry is entertaining thoughts about God that are unworthy of Him.[6] Idolatry comes when we substitute the worship of the immeasurable, real God with a god that is too small. That's why the bad steward was so far off the mark: he had a false mental image of the master.

"Left to ourselves we tend immediately to reduce God to manageable terms," says Tozer. "We want to get Him where we can use Him, or at least know where He is when we need Him. We want a God we can in some measure control."[7]

This is the ultimate presumption. But many of us live this way every day, with a conception of a God that is disposable and at our disposal. We assume He's on call, God with a beeper, but of course He won't intrude on *our* sovereign control of our business. This can seem innocuous in daily life, and we surely don't intend to minimize God. But it's deadly, the root sin of the Garden. I will manage my own affairs, thank you, and eat any fruit I want. *I* am in charge.

Here's where we come back to the question of time. If our God is too small, we will worship the creature rather than the Creator, as the book of Romans says. We'll devote ourselves to whatever created things happen to ensnare us. Sex, food, drink, money, control, reputation, possessions—any number of things can lure us from Him. Even time itself can become an idol.

Many modern Christians who find themselves stressed, pressed, and habitually focused on time may want to reconsider their image of God. If our God is too small, our view of time gets too big. It can become a menacing beast that makes us rigid with anxiety.

The point in considering the ways of the Sloth and the ways of the Controller—and all of us on the bell curve in between—is that if we have a small view of God, we *can't* be good stewards. If our God is too small, we will become distracted by idols. The Slothful Steward in Jesus' parable made his master into something minor. The wigged-out Controller loses sight of the true master by substituting herself as authority.

The notion that time can become an idol may sound ridiculous. No one would set out to worship time. But does it have its claws in us? Has a habitual preoccupation with busyness, stress, pressure, productivity, and hurry crowded out a preoccupation with the glory of God, not to mention a basic *contentment* with His gift of life? Are we missing its viable pleasures, subconsciously assuming that at some future point "when things slow down a little" we will enjoy God and the family and friends He has given us—except that mythical future point never arrives?

Again, no one consciously chooses to live this way. Believers don't intend to become time groupies rather than God followers. It just happens.

So how do we undo this way of living?

Some experts advise that better time management will cure our unhealthy relationship with time. All we need do is get "more time" (however one does that), and all will be well. Or perhaps we just need to schedule things better and stop wasting time. This seems a bit like telling an alcoholic if he'll just make a commitment to drink only between 5:00 and 6:00 p.m., then his addiction will be under control and everything will be okay. Healing unhealthy relationships with created things is not a management issue. It's a heart issue, a question of just where our highest allegiances lie.

If we say we are God's people but spend most of our time pursuing our own ends, our actions in time show our real priority. And while exhortations to be more disciplined, to try harder, and to plan more carefully are fine, all our determined works will not cause us to become passionate stewards of God's time. Only grace can do it.

If we view God as our Lord and Master, high and holy, lifted up, then we will also see ourselves more accurately, utterly small and separated from One so great. The gulf between us is too enormous to be surmounted by trying harder and leaping farther. We might as well try to leap from earth to heaven, across the quadrillions of light years of the universe itself, as serve a God like this.

The great Bridge, of course, is Jesus. He alone stands in the gap between God's holiness and our smallness. His Cross stretches from heaven to earth and back again, the huge and gracious means by which finite humans can have a relationship with the eternal God.

When Christ's Cross is big in our mind's eye, our gratitude is big as well. In that mindset, being God's steward is not dull duty, but grateful obedience. We are Christ's glad bond slaves, like Paul, wild and full of joy, pressing on to use all we've been given—including our time—in the Master's service, and for His glory. After all, we know that He will come back any day now—and then time as we know it will be no more.

CHAPTER 18

What If?

The discoveries of modern physical and biological science,
of astronomy, and of psychology, have profoundly influenced [our] conception
of the "size" of God. If there be a Mind behind the immense complexities
of the phenomena that man can observe, then it is that of a Being tremendous
in His power and wisdom: it is emphatically not that of a little god.

J. B. PHILLIPS, *YOUR GOD IS TOO SMALL*

Life and business planners often speak of "paradigm shifts." Usually this means replacing an old way of perceiving things with a new mindset.

For example, let's imagine the McDuffs, a farm family in Scotland. They have made the best haggis in the world for generations. (Haggis, as you know, is a Scottish delicacy made from the roasted stomach of a sheep, stuffed with minced heart, lungs, and toasted oatmeal.)

The McDuffs have a problem. Their sales have plateaued. It seems that everyone who is going to buy their haggis has bought their haggis. They've saturated their market and just cannot think of any new venues in which to develop new customers.

They can't think outside their box because they're operating according to a long-standing supposition that has been passed down from McDuff generation to generation. It is that no one in the entire continent of Australia will eat haggis. After all, in 1935, an Australian official vomited after eating their haggis and banned it from the country. To this very day, the McDuffs have never advertised in Australia. They haven't tried to make any inroads into that big market.

One day the youngest son, an iconoclast, decides to break with long-held McDuff assumptions. He knows that the vomiting official has long since died—not from haggis—and that his influence no longer affects Australia's government. Young McDuff writes a nice letter and mails a tasty tin of McDuff haggis to the Aussie prime minister. The PM eats it, loves it, and orders that haggis be served on the menu of all government-run schools on the entire continent. That's millions of orders of haggis for unfortunate schoolchildren across Australia.

The old paradigm—Australians won't buy haggis—was no longer the case. That assumption had to be replaced in order for new things to happen, business-wise.

Or, to change the picture, let's think about training elephants. When an elephant is young, just a cub or a calf or whatever they're called, its trainers corral it by chaining its leg to a stake driven into the ground. The little elephant can't pull up the stake; he learns to stay within the radius of his chain.

The baby elephant grows. Within a few years he's a multi-ton beast. He is still chained to the stake in the center of the ring. But now he could pull it up in a heartbeat, trample his trainers, and go live in Las Vegas.

But he stays, docile, hooked to his little stake. An elephant never forgets—and he figures that if he couldn't pull it up years ago when he was little, he shouldn't be able to pull it up now that he's big. His behavior is shaped by mental paradigms that are no longer true.

We do the same thing, though most often it involves things that were *never* true.

For example, consider what it was like when many people believed that the world was flat. They did not build great ships or dream of new lands and adventures. They did not venture far, lest they sail right off the flat table of the earth and fall quite a long way. Their world view cramped their behavior, and they were shackled close to home by false suppositions.

But then those who studied the facts and dared to believe them threw out bogus assumptions. They ventured out, sailed away across the great round globe, and discovered new worlds. Their change in paradigm changed their behavior and their subsequent outcomes.

Here's the relevant question for us. It's a paradigm buster.

What if the way that you and I have habitually thought about time our entire lives is in fact as limiting as the way people used to think about the shape of the earth?

What if there is a different way to perceive time, a way that has the distinct virtue of being true—a way that can help open a whole new way to live?

Those who sailed away on the round globe in olden times brought home rich treasures from the new worlds they discovered. Similarly, those who regard time through the lens of its science can mine new riches in their biblical understanding of God Himself. If time is elastic enough, and God is big enough, then we might even be able to get out of our usual boxes and bid anxiety and stress farewell. Wouldn't that be life-changing ... as strange and wonderful as when Peter got out of his boat and walked on water?

Sure, you may say. But he didn't walk far.

To return to our flat-earth illustration, many centuries ago the notion of a round globe made many uneducated people shrug. "So what?" they muttered in their archaic English or Spanish or French. "What difference would a round world make? It doesn't affect my everyday life in the village. Hog slop everywhere!"

In the same way, many might feel that swinging from mental trapeze to trapeze in a loosely linked consideration of the strange science of time is not particularly helpful in the practical demands of ordinary life. After all, we still need to catch the train, make the meeting, get to the appointment ... of course we know there's a weird scientific explanation of time's reality called space-time, but the world as we know it still operates by tick-tock linear time.

But wait.

For the believer, there is something enormous, intangible, and life-changing to be gained by breaking with false paradigms and incorporating a new view of time.

If we can be open enough to consider that time is not as we perceive it, but its very nature is almost inconceivable, then we can be flexible enough to broaden our horizons and really contemplate an invisible God who *is* inconceivable to human experience. Thinking about space-time and the strange dimensions of quantum physics is an exercise in humility: we have to put aside the cherished notion that our tactile assumptions are "right." It can also be an exercise in discovery. Precisely because it is counterintuitive, mind-bending, and strange, considering the real nature of time can open our eyes to a new vision of how huge God really is.

⁂

What follows is a peek — or let's call it a half-step approach — into the complex and mysterious realms of astrophysics, quantum mechanics, and relativity theory as they relate to time. A whole step would take us in too far and we would get hung up in too much information, with the tremendous risk of misrepresenting not only the still-developing discoveries in these sciences but also their ramifications. Particularly in a number of areas in quantum mechanics and string theory, the interpretations of various professionals are sometimes mixed. The philosophical materialism of some scientists shapes their theories. And reports from the field are still coming in, so to speak.

In addition, we just might never emerge from a full step in, caught in a black hole from which nothing escapes, or trapped in an oscillating web of mad particles having their way with us.

No, for our purposes, a half step will do just fine. It will give us a *taste* of what scientific study of the natural world reveals about the nature of time. When God spoke to Job about His sovereignty by highlighting His creation, He didn't go into a huge amount of complex detail. He just proclaimed some of nature's wonders, staccato-style. Here's a brief excerpt:

> *Where were you when I laid the earth's foundation?...*
> *Have you ever given orders to the morning, or shown the*
>   *dawn its place, ...*
> *Have you comprehended the vast expanses of the earth?*
>
> *Tell me, if you know all this.*
> *What is the way to the abode of light?*
> *And where does darkness reside?*[1]

God didn't elaborate. But even His short, poetic overview of the mysteries of the natural world was enough to send Job to his knees: "I know that You can do all things; no plan of Yours can be thwarted.... Surely I spoke of things I did not understand, things too wonderful for me to know."[2]

In this next section, we'll consider just a few of the natural wonders of this odd thing called time. Even taking a half step in, there are many amazements to be seen. Some are strange but knowable—and some are too wonderful for us to know. Yet.

PART THREE

RE-VIEWING TIME:
A NEW PARADIGM

CHAPTER 19

The God of Surprise

The important thing is not to stop questioning.
Curiosity has its own reason for existing.
One cannot help but be in awe when he contemplates
the mysteries of eternity, of life, of the marvelous structure of reality.
It is enough if one tries merely to comprehend
a little of this mystery every day.
ALBERT EINSTEIN[1]

... there is a God in heaven who reveals mysteries.
DANIEL 2:28

We know that Albert Einstein upset time's applecart a century ago. We know, vaguely, that his discoveries showed that the rate of time's passage is not fixed but is, in fact, relative to contextual elements like velocity or gravity. For example, we know that if we were traveling at a million miles per hour, time would go more slowly for us than it would for our friends who were traveling at a slower rate of speed. We know that this fact is quite strange.

But in spite of having studied time's relative nature in school, many of us still perceive time as did Sir Isaac Newton.

There are many ways in which it would be quite wonderful to be like Sir Isaac Newton. This is not one of them.

Newton viewed time as absolute, unchanging. The universe had an unseen master clock ticking off seconds identically in all places, regardless of any outside forces like speed or gravity. Newton wrote in his 1687 hit *Philosophiae naturalis principia mathematica* ("Mathematical Principles of Natural Philosophy," coming soon on DVD) that "time flows equably without reference to anything external."

121

As physicist and bestselling author Brian Greene puts it, "There is a universal, absolute conception of time that applies everywhere and everywhen. In a Newtonian universe, regardless of who measures how much time it takes for something to happen, if the measurements are done accurately, the answers will always agree."[2]

This makes intuitive sense, and Newton's perspective reigned for centuries. Even in our own sophisticated day, when we have known that time is not absolute for more than a hundred years, we still walk around with the mindset of powdered-wig people. Tick tock.

Albert Einstein undid Newton's paradigms—though the power of his theories came not from being *new*, as if the more recent thinking is automatically the best. Einstein's theory about time superseded Newton's because, to everyone's surprise, empirical evidence showed it to be true. It has been demonstrated to be so by as many hard data confirmations as modern science can muster.

We may still *experience* time as those powdery people of Newton's day. But considering time as it actually *is* can be transformational. To re-view our everyday experience of time with a new paradigm, we need to open wide our mind's-eye lens:

• first, to get a big-picture view of the time-line of human history and God's invasion of it,
• and then to get a mind-blowing glimpse of the mysterious nature of space-time itself.

⌘

In its view of the timeline of human history, Jewish thought was unique in the ancient world. Earlier, before God established a covenant with the Hebrews (or literally, "dusty ones") and made them into the Jewish nation, ancient civilizations perceived the passage of time as an endless cycle.

As Thomas Cahill puts it in his well-known book *The Gifts of the Jews*, primitive people perceived reality as an ever-turning wheel of birth, copulation, and death. This cyclical understanding of time informed—and was informed by—a world view that said nothing was new and nothing really had significance. What goes around comes around. Their stories—the ancient mythologies that long preceded Greek and Roman myths—featured gods, heroes, and epic events, but they were stylized archetypes rather than real human beings with real future possibilities.

> For the ancients, nothing new ever did happen, except for the occasional monstrosity. Life on earth followed the course of the stars; and what had been would, in due course, come around again.... Surprise was to be eschewed; the wise man looked for the predictable, the repeatable, the archetypal, and the eternal. One came to inner peace by coming to terms with the Wheel.[3]

This "peace" turned on a certain passivity and fatalism that pervaded ancient peoples' cultural personality.

But then God broke the cycle of the wheel of fate. The Jewish story says that He interrupted time to announce Himself to human beings. In so doing, He changed the Israelites' perception of time altogether, laying the groundwork for the modern understanding of its forward motion that we take for granted.

Cahill says the Genesis and Exodus accounts in the Bible introduce a sense of linear history. The past, present, and future are a great, unfolding story, full of significant details about real people, not just two dimensional prototypes as in contemporaneous epics like the literature of Babylonia or Sumer.

> The Israelites, by becoming the first people to live— psychologically—in real time, also became the first people to value the New and to welcome Surprise. In doing this, they radically subverted all other ancient worldviews.[4]

God was the Author of surprise for the Hebrews. He announced Himself when they were least expecting Him, in ways they couldn't have anticipated. Boom. A Personage claiming to be the Lord of history spoke to a childless man named Abram. God told him that his descendents would be as plentiful as the stars of the sky or the sands of the sea.

Abram believed the Voice ... and the surprises kept on coming.

Hundreds of years later, God stunned Moses from a burning bush that didn't burn up. "Who are you?" Moses asked.

The Voice replied, "I AM WHO I AM." A riddle, a God who dwelt in the eternal present tense, yet came to human beings in the dusty details of their calendar history. Moses obeyed God and led the enslaved Israelites out of Egypt. They eventually became a great nation, dwelling in their promised land, freed from slavery and worshiping their one true God.

Even though their land was home, their hearts still wandered. They turned away and worshiped other gods, even giving their children as sacrifices to the detestable idols of neighboring peoples. They were conquered, enslaved, displaced.

Though they turned away from God, He would not turn away from them. His irrational passion for them could not be subdued.

The tempo of the great story picked up. All kinds of prophets, in all kinds of ways, foresaw the next aspect of the holy invasion. At some point in the future, recognizable by certain signs, God Himself would come. As a human being. A Messiah. *Emmanuel*: literally, God with us.

This surprising plan played on paradox: the virgin would sing a lullaby. The King of the universe would lie, small and helpless, in a manager. The innocent One would die for the sins of others. He would emerge from death alive again. He would go back to Heaven but still be with human beings in the form of the Comforter. He would come again and make all things new.

These incredible events showed that history was not a wheel, endlessly repeating itself. It was a flesh-and-blood story, with a real storyline. It had a beginning, intriguing characters, conflict, climax, and ultimate resolution. It had a real Hero. The great story gave the shape for every human story.

Jesus divided history, separating the time before His birth from the era after it. He divided people too. Many Jews now, as then, still wait. They believe Messiah has not yet come.

Meanwhile believers in Jesus regard His life on earth as the fulfillment of those ancient prophecies. They believe that God's Son lived in an insignificant area of the planet for thirty-three years, died, and came back to life three days later. On a clear morning in the third decade A.D. He ascended into heaven. They believe He will come back at a particular time, maybe tomorrow, maybe a thousand years from tomorrow.

We don't hear as much about Jesus' return or the end of time as did earlier generations. After all, it sounds so extreme, too much like fire-and-brimstone preachers of the eighteenth century—or for that matter, too much like the first century, when the apostle Peter wrote, "But the day of the Lord will come like a thief. The heavens will disappear with a roar; the elements will be destroyed by fire, and the earth and everything in it will be laid bare."[5]

The clock will stop. Time will run out. We won't get any more.

In the comforts of North American culture, it's hard to be vigilant. It was hard almost two thousand years ago. "You must understand that in the last days scoffers will come," said the apostle Peter. They'll say, "Where is this 'coming' he promised?.... Everything goes on as it has since the beginning of creation." Then, with an insight that sounds like Einstein's concept of time's relativity but came from Moses, Peter adds, "But do not forget this one thing, dear friends: With the Lord *a day is like a thousand years, and a thousand years are like a day.* The Lord is not slow in keeping his promise, as some understand slowness."[6]

We live in time. All *our* days are twenty-four hours long—regular, mundane, tick-tock, taken for granted. Yet time touches our hearts as well. We feel its passage so poignantly; we try to measure it, manage it, save it. And many of us earnestly desire to be good stewards of it.

But as we've noted, being a good steward is more than making wise choices and prudent investments of the assets we're given to manage, important as that is. Being a real steward is not just a set of disciplines we develop, great as that is. It is a fundamental way of thinking. It is an undergirding life philosophy so compelling that it determines our self-concept, our priorities and practices.

It is all about serving a God who is the author of history, the Lord of surprise, the absolute Master who is way, way beyond the ordinary flow of time and reality as we so often perceive it. Twenty-four hours are the same to Him, Scripture says casually, as a thousand years, and vice versa. Time bends. It warps. It shifts. It's relative.

What, then, *is* this thing called time?

CHAPTER 20

Intricate Riddle

꒰੦ೄ

I confess to you, Lord, that I still do not know what time is.
Yet I confess too that I do know that I am saying this in time,
that I have been talking about time for a long time, and that this long time
would not be a long time if it were not for the fact that time has been passing
all the while. How can I know this, when I do not know what time is? . . .
I am in a sorry state, for I do not even know what I do not know!
ST. AUGUSTINE, CONFESSIONS, BOOK XI

Saint Augustine had the same problem we do. Though handicapped by his human limitations, he still yearned to discern the nature of time, to pull aside its curtain of mystery and peer into God's eternity.

In Book XI of his *Confessions*, one of the great classics of western literature, Augustine set his potent mind toward the topics of time and eternity. It was tough going. "Woe is me," he railed, "I do not even know what I do not know!"[1]

At points he wondered if God even cared about his struggles. He wrote it all down: "O Lord," cried Augustine, "since you are outside time in eternity, are you unaware of the things that I tell you?"

Yet he grabs hold of God's ankle. "I have said before, and I shall say again, that I write this book for love of your love."

In spite of these difficulties — or perhaps because of them — novelist and philosopher Umberto Eco says that Augustine's writings on time "remain amongst the most modern, precise, and revealing on the subject in the entire philosophical tradition."[2]

Augustine's modernity is intriguing in light of the seventeen centuries that separate his time from our own.

I would travel in time, if I could, to North Africa in the year 398, to find Augustine sitting at his small writing table, his pen (his "spokesman," as he called it) scrabbling across the thick pages. He is forty-four years old. Head of his diocese, he is the Bishop of Hippo. Little birds perch on his back. A warm African wind blows through the open window.

Augustine wrote his *Confessions* in the twilight of the Roman Empire, about a dozen years before the sack of Rome by the Goths. He died when his own city was under siege by the Vandals. He wrote before King Arthur lived in ancient Britain, before Mohammed, Charlemagne, the Vikings, Genghis Khan, Galileo, Shakespeare, Mozart ... before the Crusades, the Black Plague, the Renaissance, the Reformation ... long before ships set sail for the New World and stargazers mapped new worlds beyond our galaxies ... one thousand seven hundred years ago, an enormous canyon of time between his day and ours.

But the gulf between us makes our similarities all the more striking. When we wrestle with the fundamental questions of the soul, perhaps we're not so different from those who have gone before.

"What is time?" Augustine wrote. "Provided that no one asks me, I know. If I want to explain it to an inquirer, I do not know."

"My mind is on fire to understand this most intricate riddle," he went on. "It is a problem at once so familiar and so mysterious." The paragraphs that follow read like a wrestling match as Augustine alternates between joy and despair, wonder and struggle. Throughout, he talks to God, praying earnestly for wisdom and insight. And occasionally, Augustine dialogues with Augustine, which should reassure any of us who have found ourselves talking to ourselves.

"It is in you, O my mind!" he erupts at one point, sounding just a little like a resident in a mental-health facility. "Do not interrupt me! Do not interrupt *yourself* with the noisy mobs of your prejudices!"

Augustine starts his discussion of time at the beginning, focusing on Creation itself. He cites a joke that was old even in his day: What did God do before He made heaven and earth? Why, of course, He was preparing hell for those who ask such questions.

That aside, time began with Creation, Augustine says. God created time as we know it. God was before time, but it was not in time that He preceded it. God is in eternity, unchanging, supreme in a never-ending present. When people ask what God was doing before Creation—"then"—well, there was no time. No "then." Then.

Regarding our human experience of time, we think that we measure its flow. But we don't really know what it is. We perceive it as past, present, and future. But logically speaking, the past, by definition, is gone. It cannot be measured: it no longer exists. Similarly, the future has not yet come into being. It does not exist. And the present cannot be caught: as soon as we say this is *now*, the moment is past, and therefore nonexistent.

Hmm, Augustine says in Latin. *Hummus.* He munches a crust of bread dipped in chickpea spread. Yet still, he thinks, in our everyday experience, of course we measure time. Certain experiences are long, we say, or short. But if the past is no more, the future is not yet, and the present can't be held, what then are we measuring?

Here Augustine pauses to dialogue with his brain for a moment. He emerges from the conversation with the masterstroke. He relates how his long-lost boyhood, though it no longer exists, is still real, for it exists in his memory. He cites how any of us can look at the first glimmers of a day's new dawn and reliably tell what will happen next. We remember our experience of yesterday, and the day before, and the day before that, like beads knotted on a long string of memory. We deduce that it will happen again, and we foretell the future: the sun *will* rise.

Ah! It is in the *mind*, then, that time is perceived and measured. Time can't be seen, touched, smelled, heard, tasted. It can't be weighed or computed, really. Yet it exists. It is measured in a person's mind, in the very seat of intellect, personality, and soul.

"It is in my own mind, then, that I measure time," says Augustine.

I must not allow my mind to insist that time is something objective.... For everything which happens leaves an impression on it, and this impression remains after the thing itself has ceased to be. It is the impression that I measure, since it is still present, not the thing itself, which makes the impression as it passes and then moves into the past.

We assess three kinds of time, says Augustine. One is *present past*, which exists in memory. Thus I can summon up images of past events, say, from notorious dates like November 22, 1963, or September 11, 2001. They persist in the form of memories.

Then there is *present present*, the elusive experience of the fleeting now. We perceive its passage by attention. Our senses take in the softness of the chair in which we sit, the light heft of the book we hold, the sip of hot coffee, the breath in our lungs, the glance at the watch. This is *now*, we think.

And there is *present future*, which we access by anticipation. We look forward to coming events, our expectations of what they will be like shaped by information and experience stored in our minds. So two people—or ten or a million—perceive the same coming event in different ways. Based on previous experiences, stored like document and photo files in the hard drive of memory, the loner dreads the same party the extrovert can't wait to attend.

The mind remembers the past. It perceives the present. It anticipates the future. Our mind informs and structures time. It's measured in the mysterious fusion of mind, body, and soul that makes up every human being. As an element of God's creation, it's not really determined by sundials or pendulums or the millisecond-splitting precision of the atomic clock. It is not absolute.

⁓

Thus Augustine arrived, philosophically—and with a radically different worldview from Einstein—at the notion that time is relative about 1600 years before Albert Einstein revolutionized modern science with the same conclusion.

CHAPTER 21

Einstein on My Mind

I am not interested in this phenomenon or that phenomenon.
I want to know God's thoughts — the rest are mere details.
ALBERT EINSTEIN

The most brilliant scientist of contemporary times showed little promise as a young man. Albert Einstein was a mediocre student. He mocked stodgy professors, cut classes, and told jokes. A dreamer, he was uncooperative about crossing T's, dotting I's, and minding his P's and Q's. (He did like E's, M's, and C's, however.) A high-school Greek grammar teacher told him that "nothing [will] ever become of you. Your presence in the class destroys the respect of the students."[1]

In class, Einstein would stare out the windows and dream a daydream he'd had for years about riding on a beam of light. He was obsessed with the nature of light. After high school, he left his native Germany to continue his education in Switzerland. Though he failed his college entrance exams on the first try, he was eventually accepted and graduated from the university in 1900 with middling grades. He wrote several papers for a prominent physics journal, *Annalen der Physik*. (His first paper, on the physics of fluids in drinking straws, did not gain him fame or fortune, though milkshake-drinkers everywhere appreciated its truths.)

A friend pulled strings to get him a job at the Swiss patent office. He doodled notes and formulas on papers he kept in a special drawer in his desk, which he jokingly called his "department of theoretical physics." His supervisor made him keep the department closed most of the time. Einstein applied for a promotion from patent clerk third class to patent clerk second class. He was rejected. It was almost the last straw.

On a fresh spring day in 1905, Einstein went for a long walk with his best friend, Michele Besso. Filled with wonder and uncertainty, he felt like he was on the verge of understanding one of the very mysteries of the universe ... but he couldn't quite grasp it. The two friends walked and talked about physics; the light from the sun 94 million miles away filtered through the new-leafed trees. That night Einstein slept deeply. He woke with conclusions crashing through his head. He started writing, and within five or six weeks had produced the first in a series of stunning new physics papers.

Einstein's articles had no footnotes or citations, little math, and acknowledged the help or influence of just one person, his buddy Michele. It was as if he "had reached the conclusions by pure thought, unaided, without listening to the opinions of others. To a surprisingly large extent, that is precisely what he had done."[2]

A few weeks after sending his paper to be published, Einstein realized he had forgotten something. He sent a three-page supplement to the physics journal. It included a little formula, $E = mc^2$. Einstein told a friend that he was excited about its potential but a little unsure as well: "The idea is amusing and enticing, but whether the Lord is laughing at it and has played a trick on me — that I cannot know."[3]

Einstein's little formula and his papers would eventually change the way human beings understood the nature of light, energy, mass, and time itself. His theory of special relativity of 1905 challenged prior notions of the absolute nature of time and space. Einstein said that time is affected by motion through space. Time is not constant and unchanging, but speeds up, or slows down, dependent on how fast a person or object is traveling.

Further, Einstein's theory of general relativity, published in 1915, proposed that gravity was caused by the bending of time and space by massive objects. In 1919 Einstein's theory was affirmed when astronomers measured the actual bending of starlight around the sun during a solar eclipse.

Later Einstein would win a Nobel prize and achieve world fame. His implications that time, matter, space, and energy are all tied together would alter the scientific landscape for the rest of human history and unleash the secrets of nuclear energy.

In his book $E=mc^2$, David Bodanis probes the shaping factors in Einstein's thought life. Though Einstein's immediate family members were not observant Jews, Bodanis says there was a residual world view from his grandparents' day that seems to have affected him.

For example, as a small boy, he was fascinated by magnets. How did they really work? Einstein knew there must be a reason that was traceable back to some ultimate design, some answer that could be found.

Bodanis writes,

> What counted was to push through to the very edge of what was knowable, and comprehend the deepest patterns God had decreed for our world. Einstein had gone through an intense religious period when he was approaching his teens, though by the time he was [in high school] that literal belief was gone. Yet the desire to see the deepest underpinnings was still there, as was the trust that you would find something magnificent waiting if you made it that far.[4]

Bodanis goes on to say that there was a "slot" waiting:

> Things could be clarified, and in a comprehensible, rational way. At one time the slot had been filled by religion. It could easily enough be extended now to science.
>
> Einstein had great confidence that the answers were waiting to be found.

Truth existed. It was discoverable ... and Einstein yearned for a unified theory, a scientific understanding that was both elegant and simple, a way to expose the magnificent order of the true nature of things.

I'll leave an exploration of Einstein's philosophical leanings and his views about God for other books. (For his part, Einstein called himself a "deeply religious unbeliever.")[5] I want to consider what Einstein's discoveries about the nature of time and space illuminate about the nature of the One I believe created them.

As William Craig has written, the predictions of Einstein's theories of both special and general relativity "have been verified without fail to a fantastic degree of precision. Any adequate theory of God's relationship to time must therefore take account of what these theories have to say about the nature of time."[6]

At the same time, we need to note that relativity as it is put forth today is a mixed bag. It combines well-grounded scientific insights with biased philosophical assumptions. Einstein—and many of today's most influential scientists and popular science writers—share a hard-core positivist ideology that often colors their conclusions. (Positivism regards theology and metaphysics as imperfect modes of knowledge. It purports that positive knowledge can be based solely on observed natural phenomena and their properties as verified by science.)

To understand how Einstein's scientific insights can lead us to a wild new daily experience of time, we need to set some historical context. Fortunately, it is fairly colorful. I had never known the history of physics was such a hotbed of passion, drama, beheadings, and intrigue.

CHAPTER 22

All Things Weird and Wonderful

When you sit with a nice girl for two hours,
it seems like two minutes;
when you sit on a hot stove for two minutes,
it seems like two hours.
That's relativity.
ALBERT EINSTEIN

At the end of the nineteenth century, scientists were the rock stars of their day. Science was the pursuit of well-dressed gentlemen with ruffled cravats. Their lectures were attended by fans and fainting ladies; there was a certain prestige to their role, and a presumption on the part of many that the universe had divulged most of its secrets.

As Bill Bryson says, "if a thing could be oscillated, accelerated, perturbed, distilled, combined, weighed, or made gaseous they had done it, and in the process produced a body of universal laws so weighty and majestic that we still tend to write them out in capitals." The Industrial Revolution had put many of those laws to work, and the "whole world clanged and chuffed with the machinery and instruments that their ingenuity had produced. Many wise people believed that there was nothing much left for science to do."[1]

Born in 1879, Einstein was a product of this century, but he was famously iconoclastic. The prevailing assumptions that most of the key mysteries of the universe had been solved didn't lull him into complacency. He used the facts that others had discovered about energy, mass, light, and velocity—but he thought about them in new ways.

Later in his life Einstein kept a photo of the British scientist Michael Faraday on his study wall. Faraday's discoveries about the nature of energy in the late 1800s illuminated Einstein's own musings on the nature of light in the early 1900s.

Michael Faraday was an exception to the "gentlemen only" rule of the scientific social strata of his day. Born poor in mid-nineteenth-century London, he was an apprentice bookbinder with a keen scientific curiosity. He read the books he bound, and though he was not a product of upper-crust schooling—or much lower-crust education either, for that matter—he built a strong foundation of scientific knowledge. When he was twenty, a visitor to the bookshop gave him tickets to a series of lectures at the Royal Institution. One of the most famous figures of his day, Sir Humphry Davy, was speaking on electricity and the hidden powers of energy lurking all over the universe.

Faraday took careful notes on Davy's lectures. After the series he bound them beautifully, along with precise illustrations of Davy's experiments, and presented them to the great scientist. Impressed, Davy invited Faraday to meet with him. He liked the humble young man and eventually took him on as a lab assistant.

Davy's personality blew hot and cold, probably because of his celebrity status, fawning fans, social ambitions, and the nitrous oxide to which he was addicted. (Nitrous oxide, or laughing gas, was popular in Davy's day; he claimed it had all the benefits of alcohol with none of the drawbacks.) But even though his paternal and often condescending relationship with Faraday became marked by competition and friction, it eventually provided the means for Faraday's genius to shine.

In short, Faraday discovered that electricity and magnetism were linked, that force fields radiated in circles, that energy could be harnessed. His work led to the electrical engine, to the ability to power the smallest spinning drive of a computer to the pumps that pour jet fuel into an enormous 767 aircraft. It was not yet the full concept of energy as Einstein would understand it, but it was an intimation of what was to come, because it turned on the idea that different types of forces, formerly seen as separate, were deeply and intrinsically connected.

Faraday's devout belief in God shaped his deep humility—in contrast to the many other inflated egos bouncing around London in his day—as well as his understanding of these interconnections. He believed that God had created the world and all its forces, and nothing ever disappeared from His creation. In Faraday's early experiments, he saw the relationship between electricity crackling along his primitive wire and the small magnet he positioned nearby. As the amount of electricity went up, the available magnetism would go down.

Similarly, if you measure the chemical energy in a stack of coal, then ignite it in a train's boiler, then measure the energy of the fire and of the locomotive thundering down the track, you will find that the energy has changed its forms—but the total is precisely the same.

The Law of the Conservation of Energy meant that though energy changes forms, it is never lost. And it exists, untapped, in every bit of matter.

Scientists' views regarding mass were similar to their pre-Faraday opinions about forms of energy. In the late 1600s Isaac Newton had said that all physical objects have a property called "mass," which affects how they move. In the eighteenth century, just before the French Revolution, a French gentleman scientist named Antoine-Laurent Lavoisier discovered that the mass is never "lost." If you burn a building, for example, its mass does not cease to exist. It becomes smoke and ash; it changes shape, form, and properties. But it does not vanish.

Lavoisier was quite wealthy due to his day job of busily taxing the peasants of Paris. He lived for the weekend, when he could retreat from the dull demands of taxation to his laboratory, where he spent inordinate amounts of time excitedly watching metal rust. He and his lovely young assistant—his wife—would apply great heat to metal in a sealed chamber. Then they'd meticulously weigh the rusted metal, as well as the air itself.

They found that the air in the chamber lost mass. This was because its oxygen was no longer present. But it hadn't disappeared. The exact weight of the oxygen missing from the air was now part of the weight of the metal, in the form of little clumps of rust.

Like Faraday's later work about energy, the key idea was that all the mass in the universe is never lost. It simply changes form.

Somewhere along the line of his obsessively correct measurements, Lavoisier offended an inventor who came to him for help. He looked down his aristocratic nose at the man, proclaimed that he hadn't tested his scientific premises enough, and sent him away.

As the French Revolution roiled through Paris, Lavoisier's wealth and role as part of Louis XV's IRS was enough to draw unwanted attention. But his doom was sealed in that the would-be inventor he offended was Jean-Paul Marat, one of revolutionary France's most powerful leaders. Marat denounced Lavoisier, who was arrested, tried, dragged to the guillotine, and beheaded. His mass was not lost, it just changed form.

Lavoisier's discoveries about the nature of mass meshed with what Faraday would later uncover about the nature of energy. The stuff of our universe can be rusted, blown up, burned, spliced, and diced. Regardless of what form it takes, however, the total amount of mass does not change.

Similarly, though energy might change forms, like the interplay between magnetism and electricity, the total amount remains the same. None dissipates.

By Einstein's time, scientists were used to thinking in these terms. But they also thought of energy and mass as two distinct, unconnected realms. One was the world of stuff—rocks, trees, mountains, metal. The other was the world of power—fire, electricity, explosions. There was no particular connector between the two.

Holding these two realms in his mind, Einstein didn't try to link them. He put them slightly to the side and focused on his first love, the nature of light itself. In this he drew on the work of James Maxwell.

Like Michael Faraday, James Clerk Maxwell was a scientist who believed in God's design of the natural world. A stronger mathematician than Faraday, Maxwell built on Faraday's discoveries about the interrelationship between electricity and magnetism. Faraday had shown the two to be interrelated; that electricity can become magnetism, and vice versa. By the late 1850s, Maxwell further developed this correlation to clarify the very nature of light.

David Bodanis's description is helpful:

> When a light beam starts going forward, one can think of a little bit of electricity being produced, and then as the electricity moves forward it powers up a little bit of magnetism, and as that magnetism moves on, it powers up yet another surge of electricity, and so on like a braided whip snapping forward. The electricity and magnetism keep on leapfrogging over each other in tiny, fast jumps—a "mutual embrace," in Maxwell's words.[2]

When Einstein pondered this little love affair, he understood that it made light different than it had been commonly understood. It was a wave, yes, but it was a wave you could never catch because it was constantly leapfrogging ahead, powered at an awesome speed. It moves because of the "mutual embrace" phenomenon—"the electricity part of the light wave shimmers forward, and that 'squeezes' out a magnetic part; then that magnetic part, as it powers up, creates a further 'surge' of electricity so the rushing cycle starts repeating."[3]

This process takes place at 186,000 miles per second, or 670 million miles per hour.

Philosophers and scientists had pondered light's speed since the days of Aristotle. Many thought it was instantaneous. But in the early seventeenth century Galileo proposed an experiment in which two men with lanterns would stand on hills a mile from each other, with a third observer watching. The first would flash his lantern, the second would respond as soon as he saw it, and the third would measure the elapsed time.

This was a great idea, but suffered from some limitations like response time and the fact that a mile was just not enough distance. In 1849, a French scientist named Armand Fizeau did some work with beams of light, rotating wheels, and mirrors bouncing beams back at angles that could be measured.

Using similar but more sophisticated techniques, American scientist Albert Michelson set up lenses and mirrors along the bank of the Severn River in Maryland, and in 1926 arrived at the figure of about 186,285 miles per second, which is pretty darn close to the figures computed by today's sophisticated technology.

This amazing speed is not a description, telling us something about what light can *do*, that is, it can go this fast or slower or faster. No. The speed is part of the intrinsic nature of what light *is*. Its speed defines it. Its speed does not change.

In fact, light is the fastest speed that exists in our universe, the cosmic speed limit. For reasons scientists don't understand, nothing can go faster.[4] This runs counter to the way our minds work. Of course it can go quicker, we shout. Just pedal faster, or something!

Well, no, it can't.

To get a handle on this, think of motionlessness, at the other end of the speed spectrum. It is impossible for anything to go slower than not moving at all. Speedometers stop at zero. There is no such thing as negative speed. In the same way, it is impossible for anything to go any faster than 100 percent of speed, so to speak. Speedometers stop at 670,000,000 miles per hour. You cannot have more than total acceleration; there is no such thing as 101 percent.

As you can see, Einstein's thinking about the absolute speed of light would lead to other strange conclusions that would dismantle assumptions scientists had held since Sir Isaac Newton. If light's speed was absolute, then the other components at work in the world that had been *thought* to be fixed might well be relative. Like mass. Like energy. Like *time*.

As scientific writer Marcus Chown puts it,

Space 'contracts,' and time 'dilates,' and they contract and
dilate in exactly the manner necessary for the speed of light
to come out as [186,000 miles] per second for everyone in the
Universe. It's like some huge cosmic conspiracy. The constant
thing in our Universe isn't space or the flow of time but the
speed of light. And everything else in the Universe has no
choice but to adjust itself to maintain light in its preeminent
position.[5]

As we said earlier, Einstein's conclusion that time is relative still hasn't
trickled down into most people's everyday consciousness. Most of us
still instinctively think of time as constant, that tick, tick, tick, that
does not change.

But time is relative. It squishes. Also quite strangely, mass is not
absolute either. It squooshes. Einstein realized that time would "slow
down" or "speed up," and mass could bulge and swell, dependent
on how close someone or something came to that absolute speed of
light.

To illustrate, say that you gather all your old telephones, hair-
dryers, and laptops from years gone by, as well as a large quantity of
aluminum foil, coffee filters, and duct tape. You dump it all in your
backyard shed, work with it on evenings and weekends, and build
a space ship. You hop in, call Houston, and put on your seat belt.
Blastoff!

You escape earth's atmosphere, head for deep space, and rev that
baby up. Soon you are pushing close to 670,000,000 miles per hour.
You are getting great gas mileage; enthused, you push the accelerator harder. You want to pull up next to a light beam and cruise at
its speed. But your space ship can't go that fast. Nothing can, except
light.

Now you're mad. Road rage. You push the pedal to the metal. You keep pouring energy into the engine. But more energy cannot give you more speed; you're at the cosmic speed limit.

Here's the weird part. As you rev the engines, that increased energy has to go somewhere ... but it can't make more speed. So it makes more mass. Your spaceship starts to swell. Its mass gets bigger, like a balloon filling with air. It is only when you get appreciably close to the speed of light that the connection between energy and mass becomes visible to the naked eye.

Scientists with naked eyes have tested Einstein's theory and had a great time while doing it, by shooting protons—units of mass so small that the period at the end of this sentence has more in it than there are stars in the galaxy—in particle accelerators. As the particles are accelerated to increasing velocities, physicists can measure how their mass expands. At speeds of 99.9997 percent the speed of light, the protons swell to 430 times bigger than their original size.

Obviously, if you get to this speed in your homemade spaceship, the results would be interesting, though I assume that your spacesuit and your seatbelt and your spaceship would all swell proportionately, right along with you. So you probably wouldn't even be aware that you were 430 times bigger than usual. But observers on earth, somehow watching via your homemade closed circuit TV, would become quite concerned and would schedule you an appointment with Weight Watchers for when you return.

Einstein didn't have the luxury of shooting particles through gajillion-dollar accelerators or blasting off to Betelgeuse in his backyard space shuttle. But he had everything he needed to figure out that the speed of light is the connector between energy's domain of all those crackling, electrical dynamics in the universe and mass's domain of all the stuff in the universe.

Since nothing in normal life is moving anywhere near the speed of light, we don't see how this relationship, or the odd nature of time, really works in day-to-day existence. But these strange facts are real.

When Einstein wrote his famous equation, $E = mc^2$, he was saying, most basically, that mass (m) and energy (E) are two forms of the same thing. Energy is liberated matter, and matter is energy waiting to happen. The amount of energy available in any given bit of matter—a stone, a Tootsie Roll, an atom—is the product of the matter's mass multiplied by the fastest velocity imaginable. That would be the speed of light or c. Squared.

The reason that Einstein squared the speed of light had to do with the nature of energy. When something is moving four times as fast as something else, it doesn't have four times the energy but *16 times* the energy—in other words, that figure is squared. So the speed of light squared is the conversion factor that decides just how much energy lies within your Tootsie Roll. And because the speed of light squared is a huge number—90,000,000,000 (km/sec)^2—there is incredible, bulging, enormous energy in even tiny bits of matter.

If you could release it, the resulting energy is by definition moving at the speed of light. Pure energy is electromagnetic radiation—whether light or X-rays or whatever—and electromagnetic radiation travels at a constant speed of 186,000 miles per second.

For example, if you could turn every one of the atoms in a paper clip into pure energy—leaving no mass whatsoever—the paper clip would yield the power of 18 kilotons of TNT. On Earth, however, there is no practical way to convert a paper clip or any other object entirely to energy. It would require temperatures and pressures greater than those at the core of the sun.[6]

Similarly, as Bill Bryson says,

> You may not feel outstandingly robust, but if you are an average-sized adult you will contain within your modest frame no less than 7 x 10 to the eighteenth power joules of potential energy—enough to explode with the force of thirty very large hydrogen bombs, assuming you knew how to liberate it and really wished to make a point.[7]

Einstein's work led to colossal ramifications for destructive power, human history, and the future of the planet. World War II unfolded in the midst of a desperate race between scientists in the U.S. and in Germany to unleash the power of the atom, with the eventual nightmare force of the atomic bombs unleashed over Japan. In the first bomb that exploded over Hiroshima, just .6 grams of mass — about the weight of a drop of water — converted into energy, was enough to destroy an entire city.[8]

⌒∽

Now, if Einstein's musings showed that *mass* was relative to the speed of light, they also of course showed that *time* is relative to the speed of light. Here's a basic illustration of what Einsteinian flextime looks like.

Back at our backyard spaceship, you've worked on that baby on weekends, polished its shiny hubcaps, and blasted off to infinity and beyond, just like Buzz Lightyear, but different. You decide to put your spaceship on cruise control so you can catch up on your emails and whatnot. You set your speedometer on 99.99 percent of the speed of light.

You've MapQuested some destinations in Earth's neighborhood in our little corner of the solar system, and you've locked in the coordinates of the closest star system to us, besides the Sun. Proxima Centauri is a red dwarf star about 25.2 trillion (a 25 with 12 zeroes after it) miles away. Never mind that it would take NASA's space shuttle 160,000 years to reach it. Your backyard spaceship is faster.

So, traveling at your cruise-control speed of almost 670,000,000 miles per hour, you not only respond to all your email, but you snooze, eat space snacks, and listen to CDs that teach you Mandarin Chinese. Never mind that you are the size of a house. You arrive at Proxima Centauri, circle it once, and head home. You land in your backyard with a big thump, narrowly missing the kids' swing set, and leap out of your ship.

You're feeling good. You're only four months older than when you left. But to your shock, and far more to theirs when they see you, your family and friends are all almost twenty-four years older. You are Rip Van Winkle, and they are vexed.

Since you have been traveling at such a high velocity, almost at the speed of light, time has slowed for you. Meanwhile, the rest of us have been moving along on earth at our usual speed. Since our velocity was so much slower, time has moved faster for us. We have new gray hairs. Since your velocity was so much faster, time slowed for you. You're still young and chipper.

Your backyard spaceship is probably theoretical, however.

A well-known experiment in 1971 demonstrates in a small, slow way how relativity really does work on big, fast levels. Using atomic clocks that could measure billionths of a second, two scientists named Joseph Hafele and Richard Keating put one on a jet that circled the globe, traveling at 600 miles per hour. The brother clock was left at a stationary spot on the ground. Both clocks were set at precisely, and we mean *precisely*, the same time.

When the clock flown around the world returned to the spot where the other clock was, their times were no longer the same. The clock that had been on the jet was behind by a few billionths of a second—just as Einstein's theories would predict. If the jet had traveled faster, its clock would have been even more behind the earth clock. The closer one approaches the speed of light, the more slowly time goes by.

Though Einstein's discoveries are a century old, and though they've been scientifically proven as much as anything can be "proved," to 99.99999999999999 percent, they are still so strange that many of us still have not digested them. It's comforting to know that professional physicists don't take relativity for granted either. Brian Greene says, "The relativity of space and time is a startling conclusion. I have known about it for more than twenty-five years, but even so, whenever I quietly sit and think it through, I am amazed."[9]

Just as it is quite difficult to really believe there is enormous energy lurking in a paper clip, it is tough to suspend our usual beliefs to understand what relativity theories really mean about time.

On a popular level, however, the notion of bendable time is quite fun.

CHAPTER 23

Stranger Than Fiction

*Time is the very lens through which ye see—small and clear,
as men see through the wrong end of a telescope—something that would
otherwise be too big for ye to see at all. That thing is Freedom: the gift
whereby ye most resemble your Maker are yourselves part of eternal reality.*
C. S. LEWIS, THE GREAT DIVORCE

One summer our family devoted ourselves to time travel ... theoretically speaking. We rented every movie we could think of that dealt with this topic. There are quite a few.

One is the old tear-jerker *Somewhere in Time*, in which a young Christopher Reeve plays a handsome playwright. One evening he is approached by a mysterious old woman who gives him a gold watch and hauntingly murmurs "come back to me!" before she disappears into the night. Intrigued, he eventually discovers that she is a renowned actress who had been in her prime in the late 1890s. Back then she had spent her summers performing at a lavish Victorian resort theatre.

Christopher Reeve becomes more and more obsessed with this shadowy woman. He reads up on time travel. He buys period clothing and artifacts from an antique shop. He books a room at the old resort. There, through the power of his mind and the prompts of these vintage props, he travels back in time to meet the actress in her gorgeous youth, where she is played by a young Jane Seymour.

Chris and Jane fall in love, have adventures, and are set to live happily ever after in the nineteenth century. Then, in a light moment Chris pulls a twentieth-century coin out of the depths of his vintage pants pocket. Unexpectedly, tragically, the modern coin breaks his mindset that he is in the past. He catapults, sadly, back to his present. He tries and tries to travel back, but can't. Broken-hearted, he eventually dies ... and joins his lover in death, a white and glimmery realm where people evidently wear 1890s clothing.

Or there's the classic *Back to the Future* and its progressively cheesy sequels, in which a young Michael J. Fox goes back to his parents' youth in order to ensure that they get together so he will eventually be born. The time-travel device in this instance is not willpower, but a souped-up DeLorean sports car that goes really fast and cuts through time dimensions to go back to the 1950s.

Or there's a more recent film, *Timeline*, in which buff and beautiful young archeological students whose project is funded by a shady high-tech firm have to rescue some of their colleagues who've inadvertently three-dimensionally "faxed" themselves back to the fourteenth century.

The students discover that medieval times were really nasty and brutish. They land in the middle of a French siege of an English fort; some of their friends are killed by arrows, axes, and swords. Also, less realistically, all the fourteenth century people have lovely, even white teeth and great hair, so the head student falls in love with a willowy young French lass and elects to stay behind when everyone else returns to the twenty-first century.

Then there are various versions of H. G. Wells' *Time Machine* story. These involve a complicated whirligig apparatus with dials, switches, and many rotating parts. This machine can move people forward and backward in time, though going anywhere besides now is pretty dangerous since blue savages called Morlocks are running amok, consuming humans in both the distant past as well as the ominous future.

There's also *Contact*, in which Jodi Foster gets all banged up zipping through wormholes to get to a place where she can see her dead father again. *The Butterfly Effect* is a troubling film in which a young man tries to "fix" the past for the good of the girl he loves. But every time he goes back to make things "right," they go horribly, and violently, wrong.

Time travel is the staple of bestsellers like *The Time Traveler's Wife* or classic science fiction like that of Ursula LeGuin or the occasional wrinkles in time in the Harry Potter series.

All these are just the tip of the fictional time-travel iceberg, which shows no sign of melting. Audiences love the idea of experiencing periods of history other than our own.

So do teachers. Our daughter recently took a standardized English essay test at school. Students were to respond to the question: "If you could travel in time to any historical period and bring one person back to the present with you, who would it be, and why?"

Where would *you* go? Most of us would want to stick with eras with indoor plumbing and penicillin, but the question still intrigues us. Why? The Bible says that we all have eternity in our hearts ... that built-in knowledge and longing for something so far beyond our own experience in the here and now, whatever "now" is. So we dream of chatting with Caesar or Cleopatra or C. S. Lewis ... or Good King Wenceslas, since we've sung about him every Christmas our entire lives and still don't know who he was.

Though time is so basic, so tick-tock ordinary in our world full of clocks and calendars, it fascinates us to toy with it and probe it. We long for a time when the past is as accessible as the present, when we can explore the possibilities that beckon just at the edge of our rational "oh, no, that's not possible" minds.

Some of us have that feeling we can't quite shake that if we could just find a rabbit hole like Alice in Wonderland — or perhaps a wormhole in the fabric of time — we really could soar to "worlds unknown," as the eighteenth century hymn writer put it.

Time is quite amenable to such explorations. But its truth is far stranger than the fun fantasies of fiction.

For hundreds of years, telescopes have served as the most basic real-life time-travel equipment. From the Dutch astronomers who peered through the first little optical "seeing tubes" in 1608 to today's cosmologists, looking heavenward transports us. The furthest objects the Hubble space telescope has reported are galaxies well over 12 billion light years away. In other words, the light we see from them has taken 12 billion years to reach the Hubble. That is a long way to look back in time.

Meanwhile NASA is working on Hubble's successor, the James Webb space telescope, or JWST, which is scheduled for launch in June 2013. Our daughter's soccer coach, a multitalented, great guy named Ray, is one of the project's lead engineers.

In between soccer drills Ray tells me that the JWST is designed to study the earliest galaxies and some of the first stars formed after the universe came into existence. It will orbit about a million miles from the Earth, with a 20-foot diameter mirror and a sunshield the size of a tennis court. Its humble task is to determine, uh, the shape of the universe, explain the formation of galaxies, research the birth and formation of stars, determine how planetary systems interact and how the universe built up its present chemical composition, as well as see just how much Dark Matter—the unseen stuff that is a part of the matter of galaxies—is lurking somewhere out there.

But you don't need a multi-billion-dollar telescope with a 20-foot reflecting mirror to look back in time. A human eye will do it just fine.

As you know, light travels at nearly 186,000 miles per second, or 670 million miles per hour, or about 5.9 trillion miles in a year. So even when we look at our sun, 94 million miles away—although we know full well not to look straight at the sun, because our mothers told us not to—we don't see it as it is at this moment but as it was eight minutes ago. It takes that long for its light to travel to earth. If the sun was extinguished by some giant candlesnuffer, we wouldn't have any idea for eight oblivious minutes, and then we'd be snuffed too.

So we routinely perceive something in our "now" that is really not now, but so eight minutes ago. This is true even on a more ordinary scale. When you talk with someone, you see them as they were a billionth of a second earlier. We can't notice this time interval, though, because it happens to be 10 million times shorter than any event that can be perceived by the human brain.[1]

Powerful earth telescopes can look back in time much farther. For example, the Giant Magellan Telescope, or GMT, will have ten times the resolution of the Hubble Space Telescope. Each of its 27-foot wide mirrors will take almost four years to make. When it is completed in 2016, and housed on a nice mountaintop in Chile, it will be able to collect light and perceive data from the formation of early galaxies and stars that died when the universe was young. Humbling. Strange. Mysterious.

Taking the matter a few steps further, the notion of time's relativity stretches our incredulity even more. As we said in the last chapter, Einstein's theories of special and general relativity led to an understanding that time is relative to whatever speed one happens to be traveling.

We are used to the fact that objects can move through space. But there is another kind of motion: objects also move through time. Let's say you are absolutely stationary at this moment, sitting with a friend. You're both in beach chairs by the sea. The sun is shining, an ocean breeze is blowing gently; you can hear breakers hitting the sand a few dozen yards away.

But even as you sit absolutely still, you are moving. You are moving not through space, but through time, second by second by second. So is the chair. So is the sand.

When you are still, *all* your motion is through time.[2] Now, let's say you get up from your beach chair, stretch, and decide to get some exercise. You warm up a bit and then sprint off down the beach.

Now some of your motion through time is diverted into motion through space. And your progress through time slows in proportion to how fast you are moving through space.

So let's say you really speed up, to almost 670,000,000 miles per hour. This amazes all those lazy people lying on the beach. They all jump up and start shouting and pointing. The other interesting thing that happens is that as you accelerate your motion through space, your motion through time slows down. The two motions are complementary: divert more energy to one and the other will be drained of the same amount of energy.

So if you run along the beach at almost the speed of light, you will run out of beach pretty quickly, but aside from that you'll also find that your experience of time slows down. You won't realize it, because to you it will be "normal." You will run back to your un-moving friend in the beach chair and he will have experienced time "normally" as well. But he will be older than you. Time has gone faster for him since he was sitting in the chair, an unmoving lump.

The way that time "slows down" as velocity increases is one of the more accessible concepts that flowed from Einstein's theories of relativity.

This can't help but make us think of our earlier review of time-travel films and stories. Unconcerned about Morlocks, many pro-fessional and amateur physicists have explored real-life possibilities. Traveling to the future would be quite easy: all you'd have to do is build a vehicle whose velocity can reach 99.9999999996 percent of light speed. You could zoom in it to deep space for a day or two and then come back. Though you would only be a day or two older, you would return to an earth that would be much further in the future.

The only challenge in this fine plan would be building the space-ship, which currently defies human ingenuity. Once that's done, the only drawback would be that the human body is too fragile to withstand the mammoth accelerations needed to get the ship up to speed, turn, and stop.

A University of Connecticut physics professor has figured an-other way to travel in time. *Newsweek* reports that "he wants to 'swirl' empty space the way you'd swirl coffee in a cup, using a laser as the stirrer. Because space and time are more or less the same, swirling empty space could also swirl time."

Once the professor gets time swirling, he'll then drop subatomic particles into his "roiling cup of space-time and see if they're hurtled a few nanoseconds into the future."[3] One imagines particles, like grains of sugar, flying into the future or the past.

Since this plan is rooted in Einstein's theories of special and general relativity, it really does have potential ... *if* scientists can figure out how to swirl something bigger than microscopic particles in the space-time cup.

Another possibility that scientists have considered is teleportation, though this is usually related more to distance rather than time. An object could be scanned to determine its composition, then that information is sent to a distant location, where it is reconstituted. According to quantum physics, the original would be "unavoidably modified during the teleportation process."[4] So the object in the faraway location would not be the original person, but a "perfect twin." Probably an evil twin.

(This is like comedian Stephen Wright's comment, "I woke up one morning and all my stuff had been stolen, and replaced by exact duplicates.")[5]

In 1997 a group of physicists successfully teleported an individual particle in a laboratory. They are not sure if what is true for the individual particle level will work for an agglomeration of particles or a person. So far there are no human volunteers.[6]

As you can see, though time travel to the future is neat in concept, it's still a little messy in the execution. Traveling to the past is more problematic. Zipping through wormholes, like Jodie Foster in the movie *Contact*, is not yet a possibility because of the deterring fact that no one knows whether wormholes really exist or not. Einstein himself puzzled over time travel but didn't write much about it.

Meanwhile, here in the fleeting present, our experience is that time moves decidedly in one direction. People grow older, not younger. Flowers bud, then bloom, then droop. Left out on a kitchen counter, a hot cup of tea will cool; a glass of iced tea doesn't eventually start to boil. Shattered glasses and spilt milk don't reconfigure and unspill. We remember the past but we don't remember the future.

It's just plain obvious that time moves in one direction: forward. End of story.

But those who sit around and ponder such things are troubled. Why should the story end at the end? Can't it end at the beginning? After all, the laws of physics that have been articulated from Newton through Maxwell and Einstein, and up until today, show a complete symmetry between past and future. There is no reason that they should apply one way, time-wise, but not in the other.

Physical laws don't differentiate between past and future or forward or backward or any of our usual experiential labels. "Even though experience reveals over and over again that there is an arrow of how events unfold in time, this arrow seems not to be found in the fundamental laws of physics."[7]

From the perspective of Einstein's theories of relativity, past and future have no more fundamental significance than left or right.[8]

Okay, you say, this is fun, but give me news I can use. Contemplating the strange nature of space-time won't necessarily help us be better people or raise our children well or organize our closets or lose weight or manage money ... so why is it relevant?

Granted, in daily life, questions of relativity just don't affect us. We don't experience counterintuitive variations in time, mass, and space because we just do not travel at immense speeds. We don't perceive the vast distances and gravitational forces of deep space. The incredible potential energy in every bit of matter is not visible in everyday life, particularly if one is trying to wake a sleeping teenager.

Further, the scientific fact that light speed is special in that all its motion is diverted into speed, leaving no motion "left" to move through time is moot when you can't even top 80 miles per hour on the interstate without being pulled over. Any polite discussions with the police officer about how you are special because of relativity are not likely to be met with much acceptance.

But we do well to ponder, now and then, Einstein's discoveries, for they open wide the windows of our brains and allow in more light. Is it not intriguing that the closer one gets to absolute velocity — the speed of light — the slower time moves? Is it not compelling that light holds "the preeminent position" in the universe? This is "not dexterous wordplay, sleight of hand, or psychological illusion. This is how the universe works."[9]

So in essence, a being who could ride a light beam — as in Einstein's fanciful daydreams in his youth — would not age at all. For a being who moves at the speed of light, time would not move. This being would exist in an eternal now. This ageless Being, moving at the speed of light, existing in eternity ... might He, to some degree, *be* light?

"God is light; in Him there is no darkness at all."[10]

CHAPTER 24

Time and Light

Immortal, invisible, God only wise,
In light inaccessible hid from our eyes,
Most blessèd, most glorious, the Ancient of Days,
Almighty, victorious, Thy great Name we praise....
Great Father of glory, pure Father of light,
Thine angels adore Thee, all veiling their sight....
All laud we would render; O help us to see
'Tis only the splendor of light hideth Thee....
WALTER C. SMITH,
"IMMORTAL, INVISIBLE, GOD ONLY WISE"

Throughout recorded history, human beings have described their experience of God in terms of light. The Scriptures are full of light-related depictions of the Almighty. Because the actual nature of light is so tied to the science of time, it's intriguing to consider such portrayals with time in mind.

In 593 BC, an exiled Jewish priest named Ezekiel wrote an eyewitness account of his glimpse of God:

> I saw ... what looked like a throne of sapphire, and high above on the throne was a figure like that of a man. I saw that from what appeared to be his waist up he looked like glowing metal, as if full of fire, and that from there down he looked like fire; and brilliant light surrounded him. Like ... a rainbow ... so was the radiance around him.
>
> This was the appearance of the likeness of the glory of the LORD. When I saw it, I fell facedown.[1]

Another Jewish exile saw similar visions of light surrounding the God who is beyond time, the "Ancient of Days": "He reveals deep and hidden things," Daniel wrote. "He knows what lies in darkness, and light dwells with him."

> *. . . the Ancient of Days took his seat.*
> *His clothing was as white as snow. . .*
> *His throne was flaming with fire,*
> *and its wheels were all ablaze.*[2]

The New Testament records the story of this light-filled, ancient, and awesome God coming to earth as a seemingly ordinary human being. During Jesus' lifetime, the Bible gives just one tantalizing glimpse of His concealed splendor.

Jesus took Peter, James, and John to a mountain. "There he was transfigured before them. His face shone like the sun, and his clothes became as white as the light. Just then there appeared before them Moses and Elijah, talking with Jesus."[3]

Moses and Elijah had lived about sixteen and nine centuries earlier, respectively.

The apostle John carried that time-bending vision of light and God the rest of his life. Later, when he wrote his account of Jesus' ministry, he started it with this description of Christ: "In him was life, and that life was the light of men. The light shines in the darkness, but the darkness has not understood it."[4]

St. Paul, just a few years older than Jesus, didn't meet Him during Christ's life on earth. He met Him after Christ's ascension, in a blinding experience of light, in a blink of time.

Paul (named Saul at this point in the story) had been deeply religious, gravely offended by the gall of the Christ-followers, sure that God wanted him to squelch them all. He was on horseback, riding toward Damascus, Syria, arrest warrants in his leather pouch.

Suddenly something happened that arrested Saul and changed his paradigms forever.[5] "About noon," he said later,

as I was on the road, I saw a light from heaven, brighter than
the sun, blazing around me and my companions. We all fell
to the ground, and I heard a voice saying to me in Aramaic,
"Saul, Saul, why do you persecute me?"

"Who are you, Lord?" I asked.

"I am Jesus of Nazareth, whom you are persecuting," he
replied. My companions saw the light, but they did not understand the voice of him who was speaking to me.

Christ's brilliance blinded Saul. His friends had to lead this proud
man by the hand into the city. His life was changed not only in time
but forever.

In about AD 95, John, the last living apostle, saw a vision of
heaven that reflected what he had seen on the Mount of Transfigu-
ration so long before. His book of Revelation shimmers with the
mysteries of time, eternity, and the glory of the God who is the light
of His people forever.[6]

There was no human language fit to describe what the Scripture
writers saw. In describing realities beyond nature, biblical writers
had only natural language to work with. They had to use metaphors
and similes, the language of resemblance rather than literalism. They
had to use words such as "like," "appearance of," "as it were," and
"appearance of the likeness."[7]

This is all human beings can do to describe the indescribable.
Stunted by sin, limited by our nature, we see in too few dimensions
to take in the wonder of the Holy One. The Bible says that when
time as we know it ends, when a new heaven and a new earth usher
in our new experience of eternity, *then* we will be able to look fully
upon this Light and worship Him. Redeemed, restored, we will be
like Jesus, with a resurrected body and mind that are able to perceive
the dimensions of God Himself and understand the mysteries of time
and eternity.

But for now, we peer through a smudged lens. Our spiritual telescopes are too weak to see anything but mere flickers of eternity. We

don't yet see the Light that blazes from God like a thousand suns, like brilliant fire, like a radiant rainbow.

Even if we fully understand every single aspect of the strange science of time and its relativity, that still only brings us to the threshold of eternity. This magnificent God of light dwells in a realm we can't yet know. We see only a hint of His splendor.

The concept that we see only part of what there is to see is a familiar one in Scripture. The apostle Paul wrote, "Now we see but a poor reflection as in a mirror ... now I know in part." But eventually we'll see the entire spectrum of reality, Paul continued. Eventually, when we're no longer constrained by time, we'll know the eternal God in His fullness.[8]

Natural science gives abundant evidence that human beings perceive but a tiny proportion of reality. Think of a simple example, the light spectrum. This scale is a continuum of various types of radiation. Radiation is energy made up of photons, massless particles traveling in a wavelike pattern and moving at the speed of light. The difference between various forms of electromagnetic radiation is the amount of energy found in the photons.

Radio waves consist of photons with low energies. They have long wavelengths and low frequencies. The spectrum moves from this end through microwaves, radar, infrared light, visible light, ultraviolet light, X-rays, and gamma rays, which have short wavelengths, high frequency, and extremely high energy.

This range of traveling energy exists, humming and thrumming with vast reservoirs of power and potential, throughout the universe. Yet human beings can directly perceive only a tiny slice of this spectrum. Electromagnetic energy that is visible to us is but a negligible part of the whole.

Similarly, as Dr. George Smoot of the Center for Particle Astrophysics at Berkeley says, "The shining stars in the night sky represent less than 1 percent of the stuff of creation. Most of the matter created during the big bang may be completely alien to us: invisible to our eyes and quite beyond our physical experience."[9]

Meanwhile, neurologists tell us that the human brain h
dous untapped capacity. One can't help but think that af
we know it comes to an end, in the midst of eternity wl
enjoying resurrected bodies, then at last our capacity to pe
match the wonders of what there *is* to perceive.

But at this point, we see only the narrowest bandwidth
minute part of a magnificent spectrum. To use a nonscien
we experience only a smidgeon of reality ... we see only t
apprehension of what light itself really *is*.

Is God light?

Surely we can't pin down the nature of God Himself, a
be analyzed, calibrated, and clocked at 670 million miles
God is not an object.

But the more we know about the actual nature of light
the biblical use of the image intensifies our appreciation
vine. Science can be a lens that magnifies God's wonders
through it, we can begin to deduce from the creation the
its Creator.

CHAPTER 25

Science's Sharper Image

It is said that there's no such thing as a free lunch.
But the universe is the ultimate free lunch.
STEPHEN HAWKING

Here's why science's lens is so important, not only to our accurate understanding of time, but to our spiritual experience of it.

If we want to live with a new sense of peace in time, we need new ways of thinking about it—and about the God who made it. As we've said, that new paradigm comes from a fresh understanding of _real biblical stewardship_. Everything we have, particularly our time, belongs to God. God is not like us; He is the absolute master of everything. He is way beyond our comprehension. He is _huge_.

If our conception of this awesome God is too small, our stewardship will be small too. We'll fall into all kinds of traps: sloth, control, or even making time into an idol. We'll take our time cues from the hurry-sick culture around us rather than from a perspective of what lasts for eternity.

But when we see God as utterly higher than ourselves, then we're on our way to living well in time.

So how do we perceive God as He really is?

Certainly we see God through the astonishing life and words of Jesus, God Himself in human flesh as revealed in the Scriptures.

But we also perceive His glory through the magnificence of His creation, revealed through the lens of science.

Please note that I'm not equating science and the Scriptures. The Scriptures are directly inspired by God, full of the power of the Holy Spirit. Scientific study as we now know it is a pursuit limited to the scope of human knowledge and tools.

But science is still a powerful lens to reveal God's wonders. For example, we're all quite familiar with biblical descriptions of God as light. But if we're fresh from contemplating the mind-bending, actual scientific attributes of light, the familiar biblical image means a lot more than it used to.

When I consider the real nature of light, my gut gets involved . . . I am bowed by God's grandeur, shocked by the cavalier way I sometimes think of Him, scandalized by the complacency with which I often live. When we see God as utterly higher than ourselves, then we're on our way to relating all else in proper proportion.

Creation proclaims the glory of God; science shows forth the wonders of creation. Scientific information is a tremendous tool to sharpen blunted brains that need to be honed in order to perceive God more clearly.

Some believers shy away from science altogether. Perhaps they feel that its study somehow diminishes their allegiance to Scripture, as if science and faith are mutually exclusive.

This fallacy is fanned by today's tensions between communities of faith and secularists on questions of origins, creation, and design. Some journalists report these controversies as if all Christians are idiots. Some believers oblige them by demonizing the opposition and using bad science and bad faith to make bad arguments.

Natural science itself should be neutral: the objectively measured process of gaining information about natural phenomena . . . the composition of stars, the habits of tree-frogs, the speed of light, why ice floats. Science can answer practical "what," "why," and "how" questions, but it falls short on responses to *philosophical* "why?" questions. It can diagram a human heart or map a human brain. But it cannot find the locus of the human soul, nor speak to its deepest longings. Why are we here? What is life for? What is love?

On the other hand, regarding Scripture, though God surely could have issued the ultimate science text if He had wanted to, the Bible is not a science book. It's not primarily concerned with revealing particulars about space-time, gravity, quantum mechanics, or what happened to the dinosaurs. There are many issues, scientific and otherwise, that it just doesn't deal with. Believers today would not want to fall into the errors of past generations, who manipulated the Scriptures to proof-text their positions on scientific matters the Bible doesn't address.

For example, some Christians in centuries gone by used the Bible to support their claim that the earth does not move ... though the Scriptures do not make that assertion. When scientific developments made it clear that the earth was in fact the third rock orbiting the sun, some red-faced believers had to do some fancy dancing.

The Bible may be silent on some things. That does not mean it is incomplete. It is absolutely sufficient in its purpose, which is revealing the true story about God's creation, the Fall, redemption, and ultimate restoration ... an account of the love and power of God, His rescue of sinful human beings, and the great promise of living together, happily ever after.[1] Further, the necessary truths of the Bible are plain enough that they're accessible to anyone who is willing to read them with an open mind and heart.

So the Bible doesn't claim to speak to all of science. Nor is it silent on all of science. Peppered throughout its account of God's grace are also many mentions of strange things that, in fact, tie with insights on the cutting edge of modern discovery. Dr. Richard Swenson has written of this in a passage that is worth quoting at length:

> God has allowed us the privilege of living in a time when great mysteries are being uncovered. No previous era knew about quantum mechanics, relativity, subatomic particles, supernovas, ageless photons, or DNA. They all reveal the stunning genius of a God who spoke a time-space-matter-light

universe into existence, balanced it with impossible require-ments of precision, and then gifted it with life.

Does it not stir your heart to realize in a millionth of a second, a trillion atoms in your body turn over—and yet somehow God makes it work? Does it not deepen your rever-ence to realize that God is more impressive than a magnetic cloud thirty million miles in diameter careening through space at a million miles an hour, or a neutron star that weighs hundreds of millions of tons per teaspoon? Does it not give you pause to think that of the ten thousand trillion (10 to the 16th power) words spoken by humans since the dawn of time, God heard every one, remembers ever one, can recite them all backwards from memory, and even knew them be-fore they were spoken?... The truths of Scripture, the life of Christ, the discoveries of science—all should combine to lift us heavenward.[2]

Science can be a lever that inclines our souls to worship, our minds to probe the mysteries of Scripture, and our hearts to serve the One who rules time and eternity. We can thrill to its discoveries as they point to biblical truth.

For example, consider the major paradigm shift in physics of the last century. Aside from changing science's understanding of time, Einstein's relativity equations also led to strange new assumptions about the nature of the universe. They revealed that the universe was either expanding or contracting. Then in 1922 a Russian physicist named Alexander Friedmann used Einstein's equations of general relativity to conclude that the universe began in a state of extremely high density and temperature and then expanded in time, thinning out and cooling as it did so.

This cosmological theory, commonly known now as the Big Bang, flew in the face of established scientific conceptions. Physicists of Einstein's day thought in an entirely different paradigm. It prob-ably didn't have to do with haggis as did the McDuff paradigm we used earlier. But like the McDuffs, scientists worked off a presumption that turned out to be false. Their paradigm said that the universe was static, eternal, and without an origin. Even as late as the end of the twentieth century we were still hearing echoes of this mindset in Carl Sagan's popular mantra, "The Cosmos is all there is or ever will be," as if creation itself was self-contained and would last forever.

The notion of an expanding universe emerging from a finite beginning was extremely irritating to the scientific status quo. It was derisively coined the "Big Bang" by one of its detractors, Fred Hoyle, and the name stuck. (In the 1990s *Sky & Telescope* magazine conducted a contest to find a more dignified name for this theory, but it fizzled.) Einstein himself had seen that his general relativity equations might predict that the universe started from a finite beginning, and he disliked that idea so much that he introduced a fudge factor into his equations. This variable was called a cosmological constant and was designed to reveal a universe in eternal equilibrium, no beginning, no end.

In 1927 astronomer Edwin Hubble discovered that light from distant galaxies was "red-shifted," meaning, roughly, that it had stretched during its travels. This suggested that the universe was in fact expanding. As Stephen Hawking says in *A Brief History of Time*, this discovery was one of the great intellectual revolutions of the twentieth century.

What it logically meant was that the universe had to have a point to expand from, as in—oh no—a *beginning.*

Time, as we know it, and space started at a certain, specific point. Hubble's discovery, confirmed by all kinds of analysis and later more sophisticated examination, turned the prevailing paradigm on its head. Red-faced scientists had to make some adjustments in their thinking.

For his part, Einstein apologized for fudging around with the nature of the universe, calling it "the greatest blunder" of his career.[3]

Like Dr. Hoyle, some Christians don't like the Big Bang either, for different reasons. They assume that it's by definition a godless proposition. But on its face, this theory is neither atheistic nor theistic. It is simply a description of what the evidence leads scientists to conclude actually happened long ago: a sudden, incredibly powerful expansion that defies human imagination and comprehension, in which all the stuff of our universe—and the space in which the stuff resides—came into being.

This was not random chaos but intricately orchestrated. Stephen Hawking has written that "if the rate of expansion one second after the Big Bang had been smaller by even one part in a hundred thousand million million, the universe would have re-collapsed before it ever reached its present state."[4]

Many who believe the Genesis account affirm Big Bang theories as the scientific portrayal of what happened when "God created the heavens and the earth."[5] (There are differences, however, in how believers interpret Genesis's depiction of the days of creation. Some believe that the Hebrew word used for day, *yom*, means a literal twenty-four-hour day. Others believe that *yom* means enormous, undefined eras of time. Many scholars affirm that *yom* can't be precisely tied down: it can be interpreted either way.[6] One hopes, however, that disagreements about the age of creation might not split believers who agree on the key point that *God* made everything.

Scientist and philosopher Jay Richards points out that physicists' discoveries of the 1960s and '70s showed that the universal constants of physics appeared finely tuned for complex life, to the point that astrophysicist and atheist Fred Hoyle—who, presumably, did not submit suggestions to the Big Bang renaming contest—has said this fine tuning suggested the work of a "superintellect."[7]

But even when science and faith feel friendly, some believers err, I think, when they seize upon various scientific findings in a misguided effort to find some airtight *proof* for Christianity.

Science can neither prove nor disprove the existence of God. Surely the natural world supplies an abundant trail of evidence that many conclude clearly points to Him. But God has set up the situation in a way that each of us must *choose* to believe in Him or not.

If science empirically *proved* the existence of God, we would need no faith. There would be no "conviction of things not seen," as Hebrews defines faith, because all would be seen. All the cards would be on the table. There would be no choice, and human beings would be not servants but robots, programmed to make but one inescapable choice.

Science's tools do show forth the enormity, elegance, and enigmas of the universe. Science reveals aspects of time that make us more awestruck by what the Bible says about eternity. Scientific knowledge reveals beauties and wonders we'd otherwise not know. Each of us must decide how to respond to these wonders.

Take, for example, physicist Richard Feynman's exultation about the nature of a flower.

Feynman won the 1965 Nobel Prize in physics for his work on quantum electrodynamics. In "The Pleasure of Finding Things Out," the great physicist wrote about a friend who was an artist. His friend would pluck a perfect flower. With his artistic sensitivities toward texture, color, and shape, he marveled at its beauty. But, he said snootily, as a clinical, formula-driven scientist, Feynman couldn't appreciate it properly.

Feynman called his friend "kind of nutty" and went on to say that he could breathe in the flower's beauty as well as anyone. But it was in fact his knowledge of *physics* that enriched his experience. He could appreciate much more about the flower than the artist, for he perceived the beauty of its molecular, atomic, and subatomic processes. His scientific knowledge added to "the excitement and mystery and awe of a flower."[8]

For believers, scientific study can blow the doors off the way we think about the God who made time. The more one knows about the world and everything in it, the more God's power stops our breath with awe.

A friend who is one of the world's premier eye surgeons makes this point. Any of us can look in the eyes of the ones we love and see their beauty. But my surgeon friend, Jim Gills, can gaze in his wife's eyes and appreciate their splendor at a far more profound level.

He knows, for example, that

the iris is the most data-rich structure in the body. It has 266 identifiable characteristics, compared to the 35 used for fingerprint identification.

The cornea consists of five layers. In one layer, the endothelial cells are able to recognize disease and trauma at relative distances that would be equivalent to a mother in New York City responding to her child crying in San Diego.

The eye makes 100,000 separate motions in a day. The eyelids blink 400 million times in an average lifetime.

The cells of the retina—rods for dim and peripheral vision, and cones for color and fine detail perception—translate light photons into electrical impulses for the brain. This continuous exposure and development of the brain's pictures would take a Cray supercomputer 100 years to simulate what is occurring in the human eye every single second.[9]

Dr. Gills' knowledge enhances his wonder regarding the function, design, and beauty of the human eye. Since he is a believer, his scientific expertise enhances his appreciation for the cosmic genius of the Creator. It causes him to worship God.

❧

Even if we are not rocket scientists or eye surgeons, science can be a lens that shows us God's great splendors more clearly. Like Einstein— and surely this is the only way I resemble a genius like Einstein, except when my hair is wild—I want to catch hold of God's thoughts, though perhaps in a different way than Einstein meant it when he said that. The mind-bending nature of physics bends my knees as well. It makes me think about time differently.

For example, Einstein's theory of special relativity teases me to understand in a fresh way what Moses might have been getting at when he said that for the Lord a day is as a thousand years and a thousand years is as a day. Moses was educated in the royal court of Egypt and was wise indeed, though probably not quite acquainted with the special theory of relativity. But the Holy Spirit nudged him to write what he did. God is not subject to time. He is King over it.

So I can begin—ever so slightly—to conceive of the reason that God is called the One who was, and is, and is to come. He eclipses our understanding of past, present, and future ... He is in all, beyond all. He knows the end from the beginning ... He sees our stories on earth completed just as He sees us in this very moment. He is the great "*I am*" who dwells in eternal *Now*.

I cannot comprehend the real relativity of time. Even less can I conceive of this Being beyond time, this One who is not constrained by it.

So in the most general way, the study of the natural world can be almost sacramental. If a sacrament is a physical sign of a spiritual reality, then scientific study can spotlight visible representations of invisible spiritual truths. Since today's perceived conflicts between religion and science are so heated, though, it is probably better to speak of scientific study as *instructional*. The study of the natural world can yield great spiritual insights, for those who are open to seeing.

For example, astronomers estimate that there are about one hundred thousand million stars in the Milky Way alone. They have suggested that counting the stars in the universe is like trying to count the number of grains of sand on the earth.

To do that, you would measure the surface area of the beach, determine the average depth of the sand layer, and make an overall calculation based on the number of sand grains in a small, representative sample. This is what astronomers do on the celestial level. Conservatively speaking, there are about 10 to the 11th power stars in our galaxy. There are about 10 to the 11th power galaxies.

Let's get out the calculator: so, let's see, there are at least 10 to the 22 power stars in the universe? There are 100,000,000,000,000,000, 000,000 stars out there?

The largest of them that we know about (which is not saying much, given how much we don't know) is a hypergiant, red colossus that is about 1500 times the size of our sun. If it was placed at the center of our solar system, it would extend to the orbit of Saturn. Scientists call this thing Mu Cephi.

The Old Testament says that God calls the stars by name. What is God's pet name for Mu Cephi—and the trillions of other such stars?

I can't help but think of C. S. Lewis's whimsical take on this, when a "star at rest" named Ramadu tells the Narnia children that "the days when I was a star had ceased long before any of you knew this world, and all the constellations have changed."

"In our world," says practical Eustace, "a star is a huge ball of flaming gas."

"Even in your world, my son," responds Ramadu, "that is not what a star is, but only what it is made of."[10]

Does God have names for 10 to the 22nd power stars? Does He know how many hairs are on your head—and all the hairs on all the billions of heads on the planet? The Scriptures say that His capacity for such knowledge is unlimited.

We also read in the Bible that "as the heavens are higher than the earth, His ways are higher than my ways, and His thoughts are higher than my thoughts."[11] Intellectually, we all nod to the simile: yes, yes, we know that God is way above us.

But sometimes what we know in our brains doesn't make our hearts beat faster with passion. Sometimes we think too small.

For example, I realized only recently that when I thought about verses like Isaiah's, in my mind's eye I would see a Sunday school bulletin board from when I was about eight years old. There was a strip of brown felt on the bottom that represented the earth, and fuzzy blue felt above it: the heavens. Unaccountably, ludicrously, and mostly subconsciously, this fuzzy image stayed in my adult mind ... a child-sized view of God's high magnificence.

Today I can put away childish things, click my computer mouse on NASA's website and gaze at photographs from Hubble and other sources. There are deep space fields, full of flaming lights. The earth is like a swirled blue marble, dwarfed by space. Seeing it, my imagination has something real to work with. You can tell me that God's ways are higher than my own, and I believe it. But *show* me through science that enormous gulf between the heavens and the earth, and my hair stands on end.

Or consider "Hoag's Object," a galaxy about seven hundred six quadrillion miles wide.[12] It is a blue ring made of young stars with a yellow hub of older stars. It looks — unmistakably — like a "wheel within a wheel," as the prophet Ezekiel spoke of his visions of heaven.

Anyone can marvel at the stars. That is a good thing. But those who are stirred by God's Spirit can stare at the stars and sense their Source. Any fine evening we can take a moment away from the earthbound norm, step outside, and gaze up at the twinkling glories far, far away. In them we see light that left galaxies many millennia ago. In them we can wonder, with both awe and love, about the God beyond time.

CHAPTER 26

Time and
the Quantum World

ൟ

Humankind cannot bear too much reality.
T. S. ELIOT

The grand expanse of the heavens bends our understanding of time. But if we move from the immeasurable vistas of astrophysics to the infinitesimal wonders of quantum physics, we find insights about time that are just as astonishing.

And as we'll see at the end of this chapter, quantum discoveries can remind us that God's dimensions of eternity constantly interact with our everyday lives in time—in strange ways that can give us real comfort and hope.

Considering the micro strangeness of the submolecular world is less common than our macro consideration of the starry host, for it requires equipment that most of us just don't have at home: atom smashers, particle accelerators, and supercolliders. The accelerators have cool names like the Super Proton Synchrotron, the Large Hadron Collider, and the Relativistic Heavy Ion Collider. Home Depot does not stock such stuff.

So we must depend on quantum physicists. When we take even a peek into the wild quantum world at the heart of the atom, we sense in a fresh way the incredible, alien complexity of creation, including time. There are dimensions we cannot know, phenomena we cannot explain. To explore this even lightly is to realize that the universe is much more remarkable, time's reality is much more complex, and God is much more astonishing, than we often assume. Intriguingly, we can also see that the Scriptures refer to strange events that may well be quantum-esque in nature.

In the early 1900s, while Einstein was contemplating energy and mass and the great glories of light, other geniuses were considering the new worlds to be found in the microscopic arena of the atom.

As you know, atoms are the building blocks of every physical thing that exists—stars, croissants, azaleas, your body. When we die our atoms—though not our spirits—reassemble to become parts of other things. Scientists estimate that they last for about 10 to the 35th power years. Since atoms recycle so vigorously (please note that we are not talking about reincarnation), up to a billion of the atoms in your body probably once belonged to Henry VIII, with other billions coming from Genghis Khan, Beethoven, Eve, and any other historical figure who has been deceased long enough for his or her atoms to become dust, so to speak, and shuffle about a bit.

Atoms measure in at one ten-millionth of a millimeter. A millimeter is about twice as wide as the period at the end of this sentence.

Yet within these tiny atoms are scrappy little electrons, as well as busy wee neutrons and protons at the nucleus. The nucleus is a millionth of a billionth of the volume of the atom, but incredibly dense, since it contains almost all of its mass; 99.9999999999999 percent of the atom is empty space. It's been said that if an atom were expanded to the size of a cathedral, the nucleus, by comparison, would be only about the size of a fly—but a fly many thousands of times heavier than the whole cathedral.[1]

Exploring this tiny frontier, scientists in the early part of the twentieth century discovered that electrons and other subatomic elements do not behave according to the conventional laws that apply in our everyday experience. Here are just a few of the weird tendencies of the microworld that have to do with time.

First, those independent-minded electrons seem to disappear from one part of the atom and reappear *instantaneously* in another *without moving through the space in between.*

This violates not only common sense but the ingrained scientific notion of *locality*. Basically, locality means that in order to affect something, you have to physically interact with it. If there is space between two objects, we consider them to be independent. In order for one object to influence another, it must negotiate the space that separates them.

For example, if you are at the beach and seagulls are wheeling overhead, you toss an Alka Seltzer into the air and a gull will snap it up. You have affected the gull by causing the Alka Seltzer to traverse the space between you and it. (And about a minute later the gull may well blow up, but that is a different story.)

But scientists found that electrons seem to "relocate" from one part of space to another—*instantly*—without moving between the two points. And to top it off, these weird little electrons had an identity crisis: sometimes they acted like a particle, and sometimes they acted like a wave.

Second, future activities inside atoms can't be predicted in the same way that events can in the "big" world. In 1926 a young German physicist named Werner Heisenberg introduced the notion of probability to describe particle activity inside atoms. In so doing, he began a new discipline of science that became known as quantum mechanics.

Einstein's general relativity was like much of physical science that came before it in that it could predict what would happen in the future. If our planet is in a certain part of its orbit today, it will be at a predictable point in its orbit twenty-four hours from now. Equations could be borne out in real life with certainty. Quantum theory was a different thing altogether. In its submolecular world, all we can do is predict probabilities of what *might* happen.

Heisenberg's aptly named Uncertainty Principle said that an electron is a particle, but a particle that can be described in terms of waves. The principle holds that you can know the path an electron takes as it moves through a space, or you can know where it is at a given instant, but you cannot know both. So you can never predict where it will be at any given moment. You can only propose its probability of being there.

Essentially, an electron doesn't seem to exist until it is observed, kind of like the bogeyman who used to hide in your closet at night when you were a kid, except the reverse. He was only there when your parents *weren't* looking. The electron seems to be there only when you *are* looking.[2]

Here's a third weird reality of the wacky world inside atoms: Wolfgang Pauli's Exclusion Principle of 1925. If you're like me, this is just not something you consider every day, but it's fascinating. Subatomic particles in certain pairs, even when separated, somehow "know" what the other is doing. If one is in Washington, D.C., and the other's in Beijing, the instant you send one spinning, the other will immediately begin spinning in the opposite direction and at the exact same rate. If one was in D.C. and its mirrored twin was on Pluto, the result would be the same.

As Brian Greene puts it, "Quantum mechanics allows an entanglement, a kind of connection, to exist between [separate objects].... The quantum connection between two particles can persist even if they are on opposite sides of the universe."[3]

This entanglement is a connection that makes two things behave like a single, indivisible entity. It's as if at some level they know each other's deepest secrets.[4] Particles can "know" each other's properties even when those properties are unknowable to scientists.

This leads to a fourth bizarre tendency of life inside the atom. In the subatomic world, the same particle appears to be in two places — *at the same time*. This brain teaser occurs because particles behave like waves. All waves have certain things in common. If you're at the beach and have taken a break from tossing Alka Seltzers to seagulls, you can see big waves curling toward the shore. It's not unusual to see tiny ripples and swirls superimposed on the rolling waves.

This combining propensity, which scientists call a superposition, is fairly ordinary in the ocean. It's extraordinary at the teeny tiny level, however, for it means that a particle, with its wavy superposition, seems to be in two places at the same time. In experiments in the laboratory, scientists have observed situations in which the only way to describe a particle's location is to say that it is within a range of places at once.

A particle may behave as a wave. It may behave as a particle. There is no law that says what it *will* do, as in the everyday world where Newton's law of gravity lets us know which way a cup of coffee will go if it is knocked off the dinner table. Sadly, particularly if your carpet is a light color, the cup and its contents *will* fall down, all over it.

But in the quantum world, there are no such "laws" in place that allow us to "know" what will happen. Again, we can only surmise probabilities of what *might* happen.

Further, these particles come in and out of being in zillionths of a second—kind of like those brilliant thoughts that you forget, to your dismay, almost immediately upon having them.

The fifth oddity of the quantum world is this: by the end of the twentieth century, scientists were positing that these particles are not really particles, but "strings": vibrating strands of energy that oscillate in ten dimensions. These strings are like vibrating, rotating rubber bands. As the first split second of the universe's existence they were stretched because of enormously high temperatures ... now they are contracted to such a degree that they behave like points. These strings are typically about a hundred billion billion times smaller than a proton, and you already know you can fit 500,000,000,000 protons into the dot of an i.

String people posit that the cosmos experienced a dimensional "split" an instant after creation began. At this micromoment, the eleven-dimensional expanding universe divided into two: a six-dimensional piece that quit expanding—or "uncurling"—and never produced matter, and a four-dimensional piece that became our familiar dimensions of length, width, height, and time. This system continued to expand and eventually produced the stuff of the whole universe. Even as we speak, the six—at least—other unknown dimensions are still "curled up" everywhere, right within our familiar world.[5] As Brian Greene says, "As we don't see these extra dimensions, superstring theory is telling us that *we've so far glimpsed but a meager slice of reality.*" [Emphasis his.][6]

⟨≈⟩

Even though most of us aren't privy to such outlandish fun as observing the activity of particles with exotic names like quarks, leptrons, gluons, or bosons, it's intriguing to peek into this weird world of quantum physics. Like the counterintuitive veracities of space-time, but even stranger, quantum realities turn our minds inside out.[7]

This can be quite uncomfortable. Like the rest of us, physicists like simplicity, beauty, a natural sort of resonance. Einstein, who spent the second half of his life searching for a grand unified theory that would marry the physics of the very large with the physics of the very small, hated a number of things about quantum mechanics, particularly its unresolvability in the sense that some things were forever unknowable and random. Using a nonscientific term, Einstein called quantum physics "spooky."

And as Bill Bryson says, the notion that one particle could instantaneously influence another particle trillions of miles away violated the special theory of relativity, which says that nothing goes faster than the speed of light. Notes Bryson, "No one, incidentally, has ever explained how the particles achieve this feat. Scientists have dealt with this problem, according to the physicist Yakier Aharanov, 'by not thinking about it.' "[8]

As we all know, denial is handy. But physicists affirm that quantum physics will undergird an accurate twenty-first-century picture of reality. This strange understanding of the cosmos "has been verified through decades of fantastically accurate experiments … the Newtonian cosmic clock, even with its Einsteinian updating … is demonstrably *not* how the world works."[9]

These observations are just the tip of the quantum iceberg. But it's important to consider this weird quantum world because it reinforces the understanding that time itself is actually quite different than we usually think of it.

Also, in today's marketplace of ideas, believers need to remember that quantum theory doesn't stop with just being a pragmatic premise about "how the world works," as if the world is a locomotive or a toaster. It inescapably becomes entangled with questions about the nature of reality itself and thus connects with the deepest spiritual questions inside all of us.

Many Buddhists, New Agers, and others have latched onto quantum ideas as a way of validating eastern religions' beliefs that human consciousness and the physical world are not distinct entities. Here's a representative quote from an article called "Hinduism and Quantum Physics":

> What we call physical reality, the external world, is shaped—to some extent—by human thought. The lesson is clear; we cannot separate our own existence from that of the world outside. We are intimately associated not only with the earth we inhabit, but with the farthest reaches of the cosmos.[10]

This perspective is championed in the movie *What the [Bleep] Do We Know?* which is a popular-level pseudo-docudrama about quantum physics. It features a newly divorced photographer, played by actress Marlee Matlin, who is having a very bad day. Then she starts encountering Alice in Wonderland rabbit-hole experiences that teach her reality is tenuous and that she has the ability to create her own destiny.

Her story is punctuated by commentary from various physicists, doctors, theologians, and thinkers. In the beginning of the film these appear to be objective observers, though they are not identified. By the end, when we're given the experts' names, it's evident that the majority are on the same New Age page. A little research tells us that several are devotees of the teachings of the 35,000-year-old spirit-master Ramtha, a "wisdom warrior" from the lost continent of Atlantis. We know about Ramtha because his spirit is channeled through a woman named J. Z. Knight, who conducts costly seminars sharing Ramtha's insights. Our final clue that the film is weighted toward Ramtha's perspective is that one of the featured experts is J. Z. Knight/Ramtha herself/himself.

This film is available at your local Blockbuster. It's a cocktail: a splash of quantum ideas, a dash of dubious medical information, and a swirl of assertions that human beings can reject the "backwater" concept of the Judeo-Christian God, shape their own reality, and realize that we are *all* gods.

What the [Bleep] Do We Know? is fairly spurious. But actual quantum theory tends to elicit mainstream questions about Christianity's central claims. For example, a friend told me the other day how a coworker had challenged his faith. How can Christianity claim there is ultimate truth, the colleague had asked, if quantum physics suggests that there is no such thing as ultimate reality? (Actually, the probability wave doesn't preclude ultimate reality; it's a perfectly good representation of "what is," as in the truth about reality is that reality can't be predicted. This notion just seems weird to us, since we like things to be how we perceive them to be.)

As we said earlier, the Bible is not a physics text. But if we find ourselves tempted to draw from modern physics—or its trickle-down in people's conclusions—the philosophical assertion that there is no truth, that all is relative, then we must defer to the words of Jesus: "I am the way and the truth and the life."[11]

Truth is a Person. Truth is God Himself, the Eternal One who spoke this lovely, strange world and all its particles into play, the One who came to earth to save us. The second we start to confuse the creation and the Creator, as if God and ourselves and the universe are all the same, is the second we exchange the truth of God for a lie.

So what do we make of the odd gyrations of the particle world? And what *is* reality, anyway? And when are we going to get back to the topic of time?

Lest we give up on all this and go eat an entire cheesecake, this is not just impractical pseudo-philosophical discussion that has nothing to do with ordinary life. We all deal in a multilayered experience of "reality" every day, particularly in terms of our perception of time. Often we don't notice it ... but sometimes, particularly in moments of great joy or great loss, we become aware of multiple levels, or dimensions, of entangled strands of reality that cannot be neatly explained.

A recent tragedy made me think of this.

A week ago a police officer in my county was shot and killed by a mentally troubled teenager. She was a detective, an eight-year veteran of the Fairfax County police department. Her murder was the first in the history of the force.

The officer's name was Vicky Armel. She was forty years old, vivacious, blonde-haired, and blue eyed. Her husband is a police officer as well. Their children are just five and seven years old.

Vicky was at her police station last Monday when a report came in of a carjacking a few miles away. She volunteered to investigate the report and left the station to walk through the parking lot toward her vehicle. Crouched between two cars nearby, waiting for random officers, was the carjacker, a mentally ill eighteen-year-old wearing battle fatigues and carrying seven guns.

He opened fire on a policeman who had just gotten off duty and was sitting in his cruiser. Vicky shot at the assailant, trying to save her buddy. The teenager took her down in a barrage of assault weapon fire. He was then killed by other policemen in the fierce gun battle that followed.[12]

Vicky's memorial service was yesterday, as I write. By the time you read this it will be a year in the past, or longer, a thousand yesterdays away. Nearly ten thousand police officers, public officials, friends, and family members packed out McLean Bible Church in northern Virginia, the only local church big enough to hold the crowds. Hundreds of officers in crisp dress blues, their golden shields banded in black, stood at attention as the casket arrived. A policeman bent to tie Vicky's son's small shoe as the little boy watched six officers carry his mother's flag-draped coffin. Meanwhile motorcycles, police cars, fire engines, and helicopters waited for the solemn procession to the cemetery. People lined the highways to express their sorrow. The police station where Vicky was killed was covered with flowers and testimonials about her legacy.

During the service, Vicky's pastor told the congregation about the tremendous paradigm shift that she had experienced just two years earlier when, much to her own surprise, she committed her life to Christ. "But you don't have to hear it from me," he concluded. "I want you to hear it from Vicky Armel in her own voice."

Then the lights dimmed, and Vicky addressed her funeral. A year earlier, she had given her testimony at her home church on Easter morning. That talk had been recorded ... and now the big video screens throughout the enormous worship center flashed up a large color photograph of the slain officer, vibrant in a pink shirt, her blue eyes sparkling, and a smile on her face.

The audio began. "My name is Vicky Armel," she said. " ... and if you had told me last year that I'd be standing in front of hundreds of people talking about Jesus Christ, I'd say, 'You're crazy.'"

Vicky went on to tell how she'd always been skeptical of faith, that her idea of Christianity was the little old ladies who came into the county jail and the inmates took advantage of them. Early in her law enforcement career, she worked the street. She investigated many crime scenes. She saw the aftermath of homicides and suicides. Never once did one of those corpses get up, alive again. "So I could not entertain the resurrection of Jesus," she said.

But Vicky had some colleagues who were believers, and one in particular kept trying to talk with her about faith. She'd hold up her hand, palm up. "Stop! I don't want to hear it."

But the Holy Spirit does strange things—and eventually, during a long car ride to another state for a long stakeout, Vicky was willing to listen to her colleague. He told her about Jesus—not the plastic Jesus she had no interest in, but the real Jesus of the Bible. She asked questions. She was on the case. Eventually she was even willing to come to church.

Good detective that she was, Vicky Armel went to the crux of the investigation: the Resurrection. She examined the evidence, considered the eyewitness reports from the New Testament. She came to the point of decision: "He did die. He was put in a tomb. And He was resurrected after three days."

That was the clincher. "I dedicated my life to Christ," she said.

Vicky was baptized. She studied the Scriptures in a home fellowship group. She volunteered at church. Then, reluctantly, she agreed to give her testimony publicly "because there is probably a Vicky or a Victor out there ... someone who is searching for God ... and I hope that my story might help you find Him."[13]

Picture the funeral scene. There were thousands of weeping people in the pews of the enormous church. Before them were the big, bold photographs of the woman they loved. Her voice was in their ears. Her closed coffin was before their eyes.

It is in moments like these that we perceive a little more clearly how paradoxical and "illogical" are the tangled perceptions we call reality.

On one hand, the one we love is no more. The loss is awful.

At the same time, his or her life is real. At Vicky's funeral, her friends smiled as they listened to her tape; they laughed and cried as she told her story. Her image smiled down at everyone from the video screens. And though her voice was merely the modulated frequencies of an audio recording, and her picture was just the projection of pixels on a screen, she was real ... in the sense that she is vivid in the memories of her loved ones. Her unique character, her personality, her individuality, her *life*, will affect her family for generations.

As Augustine said, it's in the *mind* that we experience time: as we remember the past, the loved one's life and legacy and impact live on.

So at her funeral, Vicky was gone, dead in the casket. But at the same time she was present, real in the memories in the minds of her loved ones. We must hold these two layers of reality lightly, like a flower that will be crushed if we grasp it too tightly.

But there is more.

Is Vicky Armel alive?

Well, no. Her body is buried at the Bright View Cemetery in Warrenton, Virginia.

But yes. As you read this, Vicky Armel is more alive than ever before, resurrected by the same power that raised Jesus Christ from the dead. We don't see her. We don't see Jesus either. But we *believe*, convinced of what we cannot see: because He lives, she lives.

Believers are thus challenged to embrace glorious impossibilities. The friend is gone. But she exists in our memories, and her legacy is real. She is dead, and there is physical evidence of that fact. But she is alive, in a dimension we cannot access.

This is wild stuff. This is the Gospel. In its strangeness we're reminded that reality—and our daily experience in time—is a many-splendored thing.

CHAPTER 27

Time Dimensions

⁓

Reality, in fact, is always something you couldn't have guessed.
That's one of the reasons I believe Christianity.
It's a religion you couldn't have guessed.
C. S. LEWIS, *THE CASE FOR CHRISTIANITY*

As the multilayered reality of Vicky Armel's funeral-celebration shows, reality can't be pinned down. Even in everyday events, there is a rich multidimensionality going on, a constant intersecting of time and eternity. Reality is not an either/or sort of thing ... it's a both/and.

This is strange.

Similarly, if the science of the quantum world has a strange spin, we should not be surprised or threatened by it. Nor should we cede string theory—or any other scientific pursuit that makes us feel uncomfortable because we cannot nail down all its answers—to the ranks of those who embrace Buddhism, Hinduism, New Age mysticism, other eastern religions, positivism, all of the above, or none of the above.

I'm not suggesting that we try to construct exact connections between specific aspects of quantum theory and the Scriptures. Such exploration would be the job of people with expertise in the field.

But as a curious layperson, I do find it interesting that in the Bible we have this self-confident document that is thousands of years old ... yet casually makes claims that seem to jibe with what is intimated in the weird world of twenty-first-century quantum physics. These are claims that would have been so implausible to the Bible's human authors that they surely would have suppressed them to make the whole thing more believable and user-friendly had they not been telling the truth, under the inspiration of the Holy Spirit.

The Bible includes way too many weird, time-bending and extradimensional events like Jesus atoning for the wrongdoing of billions of human beings in six hours on the cross, then rising, undecayed, from the dead a few days later, and then walking through walls in His resurrected body.

The Bible also speaks nonchalantly of all kinds of instant effects across physical space. Think of when Peter was locked up in a jail cell in one part of Jerusalem and people were gathered, earnestly praying for him, in another part of Jerusalem. The consequence—cause and effect occurring across intervening space without a time interval or physical interaction—was that Peter was sprung out of prison by an angel.

It took him awhile to recover from this strange phenomenon—Acts 12 reports that Peter "had no idea that what the angel was doing was really happening; he thought he was seeing a vision."[1] Then he "came to himself" and walked a few blocks to where the believers were still earnestly praying for him.

Peter rapped smartly on the gate, and the woman who answered it, one Rhoda, was so thrilled and flummoxed that she is immortalized in Scripture for running away from the door without opening it. "You're out of your mind," the other believers kindly told her.

Invisible prayer, from the minds and lips of ordinary believers to the mind of God, can effect instantaneous change across intervening space. You or I can pray for a sister in Sudan or a brother in Botswana, and God can touch her or him instantly across time zones. We don't know how He may choose to do so. He is the agent of change; we are simply His servants.

In terms of Scriptures' references to entangled connections that sound rather quantum-esque, think also of the Bible's unassuming tales of wild people like Elijah or Enoch getting caught up in another dimension, or Jesus, or His disciple, Philip, instantaneously appearing someplace that should have taken them some travel time to reach.

I know, I know, people and prayers aren't electrons. But go figure. Reality is so much bigger than mere rationality can understand.

I'm not looking to find a "natural" explanation for biblical miracles. But this sense of possible kinship between the quantum world and biblical events makes me smile. God can choose whatever means He pleases to do, well, whatever He wants. It's titillating to think that He may sometimes operate according to natural laws that are little known, unknown, or in other dimensions that we cannot yet perceive, and that the design of His universe is so finely calibrated and discoverable.

Though C. S. Lewis was writing in a generation that did not yet have the confirming scientific discoveries known today, he clearly had some of time's strange realities in mind. Certainly the notion of the relativity of time appears in *The Chronicles of Narnia*, since Narnian time runs at a different rate, relative to the person experiencing it, than in our world.

"Once you're out of Narnia, you have no idea how Narnian time is going. Why shouldn't hundreds of years have gone past in Narnia while only one year has passed for us in England?" asks Edmund in *Prince Caspian*. Edmund is the type of person who gets these things.

Similarly, in *The Voyage of the Dawn Treader*, the child Lucy asks the great Lion, Aslan, when she will get to see him again. "Soon?"

"I call all times soon," says Aslan, and disappears.

Scripture affirms a created world that cries out to the glory of God, where morning stars sang together, where rivers clap their hands and mountains sing, where sun and moon and highest heavens praise the Lord. I am content to let metaphor be metaphor and don't expect mountains to sing or rivers to grow hands to clap any time soon.

But at the same time that we read such artistic biblical descriptions as simile and metaphor, we must take care not to snuff the viable mysteries of dimensions we cannot see ... the wonders that hide in the heart of the atom, the glories that shine in the fields of deep space. Creation proclaims the glory of God, sometimes in ways we don't yet know.[2]

There are so many Scriptures that tease at these mysterious realities. Here are two that captivate me.

First is the Apostle Paul's famous riff in Romans 8.[3]

"Who shall separate us from the love of Christ?" he cries.

Paul had been chained, stripped, starved, beaten, threatened with execution, shipwrecked, and imperiled in a thousand ways. He knew the realities of the threats he listed. Trouble, hardship, persecution, famine, nakedness, danger, or sword: Can any of these block us from Love?

No, says Paul. No! We are more than conquerors through Him who loved us.

Then Paul writes of the unseen world: "Neither death nor life, nor angels or demons ... neither the present nor the future, nor any powers, neither height nor depth, nor anything else in all creation ... nothing will be able to separate us from the love of God that is in Christ Jesus our Lord."

It's understandable how persecution or death were real to Paul. But one can't help but wonder: Why did he list spatial dimensions like height or depth, or time dimensions like present or future, as possible blockades to Christ's love? It seems Paul knew the universe was much larger than was commonly thought in his day, and he was covering all his bases, in dimensions seen and unseen: *all* are subject to the conquering love of Christ.[4]

Paul's letter to encourage the faith of believers in Ephesus makes similar allusions to dimensionality:

> I pray that you, being rooted and established in love, may have power, together with all the saints, to grasp *how wide and long and high and deep is the love of Christ*, and to know this love that surpasses knowledge—that you may be filled to the measure of all the fullness of God ... who is able to do immeasurably more than all we ask or imagine.[5]

We don't know how believers can be filled to the measure with God's fullness. We don't know how He is able to do immeasurably more than we ask or imagine. Like the many aspects of the physical world that we now know exist but we cannot see, we *believe* that God's love is all around us. He is closer than we think, simultaneous with our experience ... even as He lives beyond the constraints and dimensions of human time.

I thought of this when I heard the dramatic story of an ordinary man who experienced God's multidimensional love in the midst of horror.

⚜

In 1808, the armies of Napoleon Bonaparte invaded Spain.

There the Spanish Inquisition had been underway since the late 1400s. Believers and others who were considered enemies of the Crown were tortured and killed. Some simply disappeared into dungeons, never to be seen again.

As the French troops made their way into Spain, one infantry regiment came upon an ancient fortress. This citadel had imprisoned those who had said that their highest allegiance was not to crown or church, but to Christ.

A young French officer, flanked by his comrades, made his way through the narrow hallway of the underground dungeon. The men carried flickering torches. They heard dripping water, smelled mold, old waste, horrific rot. One man vomited as they approached a thick wooden door that hung slightly open. The other men pushed it further, and thrust their torches into the dark cell.

They were far too late.

A heavy chain extended from an iron plate in the floor to the base of the rough wall farthest from them. The chain connected to a thick manacle that bound the ankle of the prisoner who had lived— and died—there. His body had decayed. All that was left was a ruined skeleton, the ankle bone still bound, the back partially slumped against the wall of the death-cell. This man, whoever he had been, had paid the ultimate price for his faith.

But there was something more. The soldiers lifted their torches to see what had been scratched on the wall above the dead prisoner's body. It was the rough image of a cross. Four words surrounded it, and as the French soldiers read the simple Spanish words, they realized that this confined prisoner had somehow known the great dimensions of the love of Christ.

Above the cross, etched on the wall, was *altura*.

Below the cross, *profundidad*.

To the right, *anchura*.

And to the left, *longitud*.

Height ... Depth ... Width ... Length.

PART FOUR

ENJOYING TIME

CHAPTER 28

Counting Our Days

⁓

O the deep, deep love of Jesus, vast, unmeasured, boundless, free!
Rolling as a mighty ocean in its fullness over me!
Underneath me, all around me, is the current of Thy love
Leading onward, leading homeward to Thy glorious rest above!
SAMUEL T. FRANCIS, 1875

Jesus hung on a cross and died one Friday in human time, changing eternal outcomes. Love held Him on His cross ... the vast, unmeasured love that can deliver human beings from the chains of time when their days on earth are done.

Christ's cross is the intersection of time and eternity.[1] At this crux of history, a common thief hung next to the dying God. The very last words Jesus said to a human being before He died were to this repentant sinner ... who won heaven itself.

"I tell you the truth," Jesus told the man, at a time when every word was agony, "*today* you will be with me in paradise."[2]

Some people know when their "today" will come. The thief next to Christ knew his time was done. The Spanish prisoner who died for his faith during the Inquisition knew his days were numbered. Today doctors sometimes give terminal patients a timeline. *You have six months*, they'll say. *Perhaps a year.*

I thought of this the other day when our teenage daughter showed me a music video. I don't recall the name of the group or the title of the song, but otherwise I remember it well. It was about a guy in New York who begins to see life differently through a near-death experience.

One morning he is distracted by his cell phone and steps off the curb and into the path of an oncoming bus. At the last second, a man rushes into the street, pulls him out of the way, and then disappears into the crowd.

Shaking himself off, our guy realizes that he can now perceive something he couldn't see before. There are hundreds of people around him on the sidewalks, and above each person's head is a miniature monitor with red digital numbers. It looks like an odometer ... but these numbers are counting *down*. No one else can see them, but everywhere he looks, he sees these little counters hovering above people's heads. Most of the numbers are enormous, but whatever they are, they're all getting smaller with each second. What does it mean?

As he walks he comes upon an apartment building. An ambulance is in the street, its red lights flashing. Medics are tending an elderly lady on a gurney. She is gray. Our guy realizes that her odometer numbers are the lowest he's seen yet. The paramedics are doing all they can, but their faces are grim. The counter runs down ... 6, 5, 4, 3, 2, 1, 0. It stops. The medics pull the sheet over the woman's face. She is dead.

Now our man knows what the numbers mean. With wild urgency he scans each face as people hurry about their normal business, unaware that their lives' seconds are ticking, ticking, away. He desperately looks at his reflection in shop windows, but he can't see his own monitor. He has no idea when his time will come.

As we said at the beginning of this book, time's passage tears at all of us. Teenagers and adults alike feel its pain, though we express it and respond to it in different ways. But if God is big enough, and loves us enough, to actually save us—as He did that thief on the cross as *his* time ran out—then there is hope. Our hope in time will only be as big as our perception of God.

When we considered a bit about scientific discovery as a "lens" that can help us see God bigger, it wasn't a perfect metaphor. A magnifying glass makes its object look larger than it is. But we can't put God under a microscope, and He can't look larger than He is. Similarly, a telescope makes distant phenomena look closer than they are. But no scope can draw Him closer.

God chooses to draw close to those who seek Him. Like the master in Jesus' parable, He will return one day to commend those who look expectantly for His coming. He'll welcome them into the great "today" of paradise.

In the interim, we're stewards of however many days He gives us. And the treasure of God's grace is that Jesus not only gives us the future riches of eternity. He can also give us rich joy in the present of our days on earth.

CHAPTER 29

Enter into Joy

After a long time the master of those servants returned and settled accounts with them. The man who had received the five talents brought the other five. "Master," he said, "you entrusted me with five talents. See, I have gained five more."

His master replied, "Well done, good and faithful servant! You have been faithful with a few things; I will put you in charge of many things. Come and share your master's happiness!"

The man with the two talents also came. "Master," he said, "you entrusted me with two talents; see, I have gained two more."

His master replied, "Well done, good and faithful servant! You have been faithful with a few things; I will put you in charge of many things. Come and share your master's happiness!"

MATTHEW 25:19–23

"You are worried and upset about many things," Jesus once said to Martha of Bethany. He says it to you and me as well. But "who of you by worrying can add a single hour to his life? Since you cannot do this very little thing, why do you worry about the rest?"[1]

God made time. For Him, it is a "very little thing" to add an hour to our lives. He's just not subject to the same temporal constraints that so yoke and choke us. For God, a day is as a thousand years, or a thousand years is as a day.[2] No big deal.

If we are really connected with this One who lives beyond time, we have a real choice in how we live in it. We can focus on the worries, burdens, and fears of our own limited experience and miss the joy that could be ours ... or we can take the risk, venture out, and truly believe that *God* is the master. He is not like us. He is absolutely sovereign over time and eternity.

Jesus—God on earth—is the supreme example of time steward-ship. But before we consider His attitude toward time, it's encour-aging that we can also draw great principles from limited fellow humans.

Consider again the biblical story of the twisted sisters from Beth-any and the evening Jesus dropped in for dinner. As we've already seen, Martha was a Controller run amok that night. But her sister Mary gives us some practical ideas about stewardship and joy in the journey of time.

First, she prioritized according to eternal values, not temporal ones.

Mary had a choice in how she used her time that long-ago eve-ning in Bethany. She could be with Jesus, or she could work in the kitchen. Jesus told frustrated Martha that Mary's decision to sit with Him was better than the kitchen option. Rather than being intimi-dated by Martha and following in her steamy wake, Mary evaluated the situation and chose a different course.

This simple example hits home if we think about it in today's time management terms. One classic paradigm for doing so is author Stephen Covey's well-known time-usage categories.[3]

1. Urgent and important. These are the things that must be done as soon as possible and are truly important to our core values. For ex-ample, certain vaccinations are due by certain times in our children's lives. We can jeopardize their health if we miss these deadlines. They are both urgent and important to our core value of caring for our families.

2. Not urgent but important. These things are most vital to our real priorities, but they don't have pressing deadlines, so they often get pushed to the back burner. They usually involve relationships, rec-reation, refreshment, planning, and prevention. Spending time with God and family fits this category.

3. Urgent and not important. These are the time eaters that demand our immediate attention. They're usually important to someone *else's* agenda, not to our own true values. They clamor for our time— phone calls, meetings, emails, committees—and it's way too easy to automatically think that they're important just because they're insistent. Martha was yelling loud and urgently for Mary to come to the kitchen. Mary knew that her relationship with Jesus was more important.

4. *Not urgent and not important.* This involves time wasters, escape activities, and things we do to avoid doing things we don't want to do. A lot of computer games and television shows seem to fit this category.

If we fill our days with things from categories three and four—things that might be labeled "trivial," "okay," "fine," and even "good," regarding their real values in terms of eternity—we'll never have room for what is *best*.

But if we start with what is best, then the other things will fit in as needed. Being a good steward of God's time is always a question of prioritizing: evaluating the options and seeking what will please the King. Mary chose listening to Christ—literally—over kitchen work. Meal preparation is a good thing ... but it wasn't better than being with Jesus.

It can be hard for us today, because Jesus isn't physically present. But we have to hold firm to what we believe: by the power of the Holy Spirit, God is with us. We still can choose every day to sit with Him, to listen to Him. Or we can get distracted by seeking after other things.

Jesus said something similar in the Sermon on the Mount. "So do not worry, saying, 'What shall we eat?' or 'What shall we drink?' or 'What shall we wear?' For the pagans run after all these things, and your heavenly Father knows that you need them. *But seek first his kingdom and his righteousness, and all these things will be given to you as well.*"[4]

Second, Mary was willing to be countercultural in how she prioritized and used her time.

She cared about Jesus more than she cared what other people thought. She "sat at Jesus' feet"—a typical first-century way of describing the relationship between student and instructor. When an important rabbi taught, he would sit at an elevated level, above his students. They would be at his feet, literally. In first-century Israel, women were prohibited from this kind of public instruction. It was a male privilege.

So, though we wouldn't think twice about it, Mary made a choice that was bold for her day. She wasn't meek and anemic, as she's often depicted, while red-faced Martha had all the personality. Mary was brave and single-minded, willing to flout convention in order to learn from Jesus. Since her family was socially prominent, she had a lot to lose. But she valued Jesus above socially acceptable norms.

In our own experience, we may have to buck cultural tides to choose what is best, time-wise. Mary knew that Jesus would not be with her much longer, and acted accordingly. We know that Jesus is coming back; we should act accordingly. Just like the stewards who were entrusted with resources while the Master went away for a trip, we know that at a certain point in human time, He will return.

So we're looking forward to an Arrival that's just not on the minds of our nonbelieving friends. That makes us different.

Further, it's utterly countercultural to make the steward's assertion that our time is not our own. In our egalitarian, rights-oriented culture, the common view is that of course it's *our* time. End of story.

But the steward hears the tick of a different clock. All time is God's; He created it, just as He created us, just as He created all things. The ultimate goal of life, in every breath, is to serve Him, to enjoy Him and His creation, to revel, really, in His presence. This true freedom is only found, paradoxically, in being a bond-servant. Otherwise we end up being a slave to whatever random thing that happens to master us.

It's countercultural today to buck the obsession with hurry. "Sitting at Jesus' feet," so to speak, takes time. The spiritual priorities of prayer, meditation on the Scriptures, fellowship in the community of believers, and serving the needy all require real time investments. They can't be put off until "later," when we have more time. This is a lie Satan loves to whisper in our ears. *Later . . . later.* It lulls us to sleep.

Further, spiritual pursuits of God can't be done on the fly. They can't be multitasked. They can't be subcontracted to paid professionals. Though seemingly the least "productive" way to spend our time, our pursuit of God is inestimably more important than the many things in our lives that crowd Him out.

This is not to say that we must all move to the cloister, that spiritual peace and power don't come in the midst of mayhem. They do. We can worship God throughout busy days, in work, play, on the battlefield, in complexity and hurry.

But in order to stay tethered to a *real* understanding of God, rather than turning Him into a small, dim creation of our own imaginations, we have to use time to seek Him as He really is. Since He is so beyond us, this can't be done on the quick. Discerning the holy, holy, holy God requires concentration and attentiveness. If we grab God on the run like a bagel, our conception of Him shrinks to carry-out size. And if our god is too small, we end up, eventually, in the grip of ridiculous idols.

Third, Mary perceived the big-picture perspective.

Mary could see what was "better" because she saw further than the end of her nose. I think she understood the historical timeline in a way that few people in the Gospels did. She realized that Jesus wasn't going to be with them for long, and she wanted to soak up everything she could from Him while He was still there. While most of the disciples ignored, missed, or indulged in denial about Jesus' teachings that He would soon be taken away, I think Mary got it.

Consider the beautiful, strange story about Mary adorning Jesus with perfume.

Less than a week before Christ was crucified, He came to visit again at Martha's house. The story is quite different from the earlier dinner party where Martha blew up. Here the Scripture simply records that "a dinner was given in Jesus' honor. Martha served, while Lazarus was among those reclining at the table with Him." It sounds like a lovely evening of domestic tranquility.

Then countercultural Mary rocked the boat. "Mary took about a pint of pure nard, an expensive perfume. She poured it on Jesus' feet and wiped his feet with her hair. And the house was filled with the fragrance of the perfume."[5]

Normally middle-eastern hosts of the day would anoint a guest's head when he entered their home, most often with olive oil. The lowest household servants ordinarily did the job of washing guests' dirty feet with water and fresh towels. In double-edged humility, Mary the hostess anointed Jesus' feet, rather than His head. She let down her hair and used it to dry Jesus' feet. Women did not loose their hair in public. The scene was embarrassingly intimate.

Mary also broke open a jar of pure nard. Nard was a lush, aromatic ointment made from the roots of an East Indian plant. It was imported from India in sealed alabaster jars. After its seal was broken, the nard could not keep its fragrance for long. So once the jar was opened, it had to be used up or it would be useless.

A pint of pure nard was worth about 300 *denari* in first-century Israel. So we might say today that Mary broke out a $35,000 jar of perfume.

This shameless extravagance had the disciples shaking their heads, and it's easy to agree with them. The wastefulness infuriated Judas so much—not because he cared about the poor, but because he often dipped into the cashbox—that the Bible says it was the last straw. He decided to act on his plan to betray Jesus.

Sure, the money could have been used for charitable purposes—after all, Jesus didn't *need* perfume buttered on Him, and there were plenty of poor people around who did need food. Mary's act seemed very uneconomical ... *unless* you understood that the God of the vast universe had visited your planet and was there in the room with you, though not for much longer. If you understood that, you would think in terms of heavenly economics.

Mary seemed to know that Jesus' death and burial were just days away. She wanted to worship Him while He was still among them. She wanted to make clear through the actions of her body the attitude of her soul. She was a servant. A steward—not the owner—of anything, everything that God had given her.

Today, in terms of our stewardship of time, we sometimes miss what Mary knew. Sometimes we forget the big-picture timeline—and perhaps that's part of the reason that we don't always seem distinct from the world around us. The reality is, as the old song puts it, this world is not our home ... we're just a-passin' through. We have eternity in our hearts, and we're headed to another dimension to live in it at some point.

In this sense, Christians are in a win-win situation. When life is going well, when we are filled with wonder at this world's great beauties and blessings; then it's "all this and heaven too!" as Bible commentator Matthew Henry exclaimed.

When life is broken and filled with pain, we know that it can be endured, for it will end. One great morning, we will wake and the Black Plague of sin and death will be gone. And the great gift will not be time—wonderful, glorious time—but the eclipsing gift of eternity, with the immeasurable joys and bold laughter of heaven.

Fourth, Mary lived in the moment.

Remember: wherever you are, be all there! Mary was fully with Jesus, right then, rather than preoccupied with what would happen next.

Martha, on the other hand, was distractedly driving her mental truck toward some future point: when the meal was made and served and the dishes were all washed and the tea towels were folded for tomorrow, we suppose, *then* she would sit with Jesus. Maybe. She was missing the present of His presence because she was so focused on all the things that just had to happen, in her opinion, before she was free to enjoy Him. And of course by the future point when Martha would have been satisfied that she was indeed able to sit down—if that ever happened—it would have been too late. Jesus and the other friends would have been in bed.

People who live in the "now" are immensely attractive. It's an intriguing paradox: when your hope is firmly anchored in heaven's future assurance, you're free to live fully in your moments on earth. This doesn't mean that such people never plan for the future or learn from the past. It just means that they rest in Jesus wherever they go, free from anxiety about tomorrow. They're able to fully enjoy life's pleasures. They can be full partners in relationships, rather than pre-occupied with whatever is coming next, their eyes darting around the room. You don't have to take their head between your hands and shout things like, *"Focus!"*

Fifth, Mary left a legacy.

Mary is just mentioned a few times in the New Testament story. We have sketches of only a few hours, all told, in her life. But when she chose to be with Jesus, she made choices that echoed in eternity. She also made an impact for generations to come in human time. Two thousand years later, people are still learning how to love Jesus because of her example.

Sixth, Mary seized the opportunity to glorify God.

Paul used this idea in his letter to the Ephesians. "Be very careful, then, how you live—not as unwise but as wise, *making the most of every opportunity* ..."[6] In the original Greek, the metaphor Paul used was that of the marketplace, of alert merchants watching for investment opportunities and buying them up to extend the master's kingdom.

How do we seize the moment and invest time to extend God's Kingdom?

Our actions in time do so as they give glory to Him. We give glory to God when we obey Him. Any act of obedience to His will, small or large, gives honor to Him ... any time we whisper, like Jesus, "not my will, but Yours be done."

Further, we multiply God's glory any time someone we've touched with the Gospel receives Him. The more people who know Christ, mirroring His light back to Him, the more glory He receives.

We also shine honor to the King when we live out His rule in a world that is bent on self-rule. Christ's pleasure is that we love God with all that's in us, and that we love our neighbor as ourselves.

When we bring the peace, justice, love, and truth of Christ's reign to the people and current structures of this world, we give Him glory both now and in eternity.

There is supernatural power available for all this, if we are humble enough to receive it. If we search the Scriptures and follow the nudge of the Holy Spirit, it's not hard to know what glorifies God. Like that alert merchant, we look for opportunities to extend the Master's holdings, expectant, watchful, ready to do whatever we can to honor the King.

This is a proactive, creative enterprise. We could say that it's fun, but that would sound too much like Stewardship Lite. But there is surely deep, odd *pleasure* to be found in the riches of serving Christ full tilt, unworried about time, fully abandoned to the love of Jesus. As John Piper puts it in one of his many wonderful writings on this topic, "God is most glorified in us when we are most satisfied in Him."[7]

Mary took *pleasure* in being with Jesus. She was audacious and creative ... can you imagine how pink her cheeks got when she first thought of taking that $35,000 jar of perfume and anointing Christ with it? She boldly grabbed for the gusto of doing whatever she could in the moment to glorify God.

So perhaps Mary's story can speak to the questions with which this book opened.

First, Mary shows how finite beings—real people like you and me—live in relationship with an unfathomable God who transcends time.

There's a deep yearning in all of us to know Him. Eternity itself is planted in our hearts; we know this quick time in a fallen world is not all there is. We long for the unchanging permanence of God's glorious light and love.

How can we connect with this unapproachable God?

The answer of the Bible is simply "through Jesus Christ our Lord."[8]

Mary had the astounding opportunity to sit at Jesus' feet, to caress them with her hair, to see Him and touch Him and believe He was the Son of God.

But what about us? As Jesus said after His resurrection, "Blessed are those who have not seen and yet have believed."[9]

That would be us. We're no Mary, but we can still live in a relationship with the eternal God through Jesus Christ. He is unseen — but real.

This is related to the second issue we raised at the beginning of this book. We live at peace in time through Jesus. "Peace, I leave with you," He said. "I will never leave you or forsake you."

As St. Patrick wrote in "The Breastplate,"

Christ with me, Christ before me, Christ behind me,
Christ in me, Christ beneath me, Christ above me,
Christ on my right, Christ on my left,
Christ when I lie down, Christ when I sit down, Christ when I arise . . .[10]

Jesus is all around us, beneath, before, behind. Further, Christ is *in* us. He is with us always, even to the end of the world. His presence gives us rest. *He* is our Peace.

And then there's the third question with which we opened this book, about Moses' prayer that God would teach him to count his days in Psalm 90: "How do we make our days count?"

The answers depend on God's individual calling to each of us, whatever season of life we may be in. There are no formulas. But regardless of our circumstances, God will be faithful to urge us toward what He would have us do in time. If we have the ears to listen, He will give us what we need to do His will. We can have hope even in tragedy; we know that sorrow is not the end of the story. We can be at peace in the "now" because we know — even if we don't understand it — that our times are in God's hands.

CHAPTER 30

Time in His Hands

❦

The hand of Jesus is the hand which rules our times.
He regulates our life clock. Christ is for us and Christ is in us.
My times are in his hand. My life can be no more in vain
than was my Savior's life in vain.
E. PAXTON HOOD, *DARK SAYINGS ON A HARP*, 1865

Our time is in God's hands.

David wrote about this truth nine hundred years before Christ. He experienced it during one of the most wretched times in his life.[1] Enemies were slandering him and assassins were searching for him. Frightened, fevered, and hungry, David hid in caves, sleeping only in snatches.

Desperate, David flung his hope on God. "There is terror on every side," he cried. "But I trust in you, O LORD; I say, 'You are my God.' *My times are in your hands.*"[2]

My times are in your hands.

These simple words are like stone castles from which heralds blow the trumpets of the King. They send us hope across the centuries.

They're the same words that a dying preacher used to galvanize his congregation on May 17, 1891. Charles Haddon Spurgeon was considered by many to be the greatest preacher of nineteenth-century England. He preached at the first "megachurch" gatherings of his time to congregations of 10,000 people. His sermons were printed every week, read by royalty and the masses.

Spurgeon also suffered from chronic clinical depression. He was well-acquainted with struggles, grief, and despair. So he was no triumphal glad-guy preaching a happy-clappy, easy-cheesy gospel. He knew the threats and fears of dark nights of the soul.

In it all, like David, Spurgeon clung to God's eternal promises. He drew strength from Psalm 31. If our times are in God's hands, said Spurgeon, then we can enjoy practical results from that fact in our daily experience. Here are just a few:

God can cure us from worry about today.

If we really knew how big God is, our worries would incinerate like germs that are annihilated by exposure to the sun. As Spurgeon put it, "Tell the Lord what you feel, and what you fear. Ten minutes' praying is better than a year's murmuring. He that waits upon God, and casts his burden upon him, may lead a royal life: indeed, he will be far happier than a king."[3]

God can deliver us from fear of the future.

It's human nature to have fears ... but God's perfect love can cast them out. If our god is small, our fears will be big. If our God is as ineffably enormous as His universe hints, then His love is huge enough to drive out our fears.

"Your times are in God's hand," says Spurgeon, "and this secures them. The very word 'times' supposes change for you; but as there are no changes with God, all is well. Things will happen which you cannot foresee; but your Lord has foreseen all, and provided for all. Nothing can happen without His divine allowance."

God can deliver us from our natural tendencies. He can give us supernatural peace.

God can free us to serve Him each day.

If the King is taking care of our business, then we are free to invest ourselves fully in His business. We're stewards who can fling ourselves with abandon into God's work without thought to self-preservation or self-protection. God will preserve and defend us.

God can assure us that all is well for eternity.

Even when we come to our end, He will not let us go. We may well not approach death's transition with particular anticipation ... but we can pass through it with confidence. Like God's servants throughout the centuries of the Church, we have the freedom to be extravagant with our very lives. We can't be killed until it is God's time for us.

Spurgeon concluded his sermon with a personal note. "I have not been able to preach on this text as I had hoped to do," said the great minister, "for I am full of pain, and have a heavy headache; but thank God, I have no heartache, with such a glorious truth before me. Sweet to my soul are these words — 'My times are in thy hand.' Take this golden sentence home with you."

Spurgeon surely took that golden sentence Home with him. A few months later, at age fifty-seven, he was dead. Yet Spurgeon's words, based in King David's words of Scripture, live on. They travel across time to give us strength.

✦

Do we really believe that our times are in God's hands?

Let's return to Martha of Bethany for a moment. She faced a similar question. And though she had her foibles, she had some great moments. She clearly loved Jesus, and He loved her all the way through.

One day Martha and Mary's brother, Lazarus, got sick. The women sent for Jesus, knowing the Lord could heal him. Yet Jesus did not come.

Lazarus died. His grieving sisters wrapped him in long strips of linen. The townspeople laid Lazarus in his tomb.

As Jesus was on His way to Bethany, Martha went out on the road to meet Him.

"Lord," Martha says, "If you had been here, my brother would not have died. But I know that even now God will give you whatever you ask."[4]

Did she dare to believe that Jesus might raise her brother, as He had raised others, from the dead?

"Your brother will rise again," Jesus said.

Martha nodded. She knew her theology. "I know he will rise again in the resurrection at the last day."

But Jesus *was* theology, the knowledge of God in the flesh. "*I am the resurrection and the life,*" He said. "He who believes in me will live, even though he dies, and whoever lives and believes in me will never die."

Then Jesus asked Martha the question that echoes through the centuries, the central question of eternity for all of us who want to trust Him but are sometimes faint with fear.

"Do you believe this?"

Martha was bold. "Yes, Lord. I believe that you are the Christ, the Son of God, who was to come into the world."

Jesus' question—and Martha's gutsy answer—bring us right to the central point in any consideration of our relationship with time.

Jesus stands before us—feeling our pain, loving us through and through, more than we know. More than we can imagine. He extends His hand. "I am life," He says. "The one who believes in me will live, even though he dies! Do you believe this?"

This is not only a question about our eternal destination. It's a question for us in the midst of time. Do we believe that God is who He says He is? Is He big enough to hold us in His hands? Can we trust Him with our lives ... our time ... both of which are really His?

"Do you trust me?" Jesus asks, His hand extended to grip our own, to pull us further into the great adventure. Do we trust Him for our eternal future *and* our harried present? Can we believe that there is enough time each day to do His will for that day? Can we really rely on Him, not our carefully calibrated schedules, our best-laid plans, that house of cards we call "control"?

This is hard. It goes against our sinful grain and selfish gain ... but it can be perversely pleasurable as well. It gives an entirely different sensibility to interruptions, emergencies, and difficulties, because in this mindset *no time is wasted.*

Let's use a mundane example. Say we're caught in traffic. There's been an accident on the highway, everything is at a standstill ... and we can't get to some very important meeting. God must have been looking the other way; doesn't He know that our time would be much better used for His Kingdom if we were sitting in that important meeting rather than steaming in traffic?

This enormous God who inhabits eternity, who was, and is, and is to come, sovereign Lord of the galaxies and their innumerable stars, King of the heavens and the earth ... is it presumptuous to suppose that He cares about something as commonplace as traffic?

He cares. Jesus says that not a hair can fall from your head, nor a sparrow from the sky, that He does not know of it. If He is the omnipotent, omniscient God, then He somehow orchestrates all things to work together for the good of those who love Him and are called according to His purpose. *His* purpose, not mine or yours.

So in this banal example, if God allows us to get stuck in traffic, perhaps He is more concerned about our pliable response to this threat to our beloved and brittle control rather than the particulars of whether we make the meeting or not.

Some Christians preach the sovereignty of God yet act like the furtherance of His Kingdom is up to them. They can become so anxious about time that they regard any interruption as "spiritual warfare"; anything messy that slows them down is thwarting the very purposes of the Kingdom, because God needs them to have an immaculate schedule. This mindset can border on human ego rather than Kingdom effectiveness.

God is in all that He allows. He cares more about our character than our calendar. He allows interruptions in our plans. He allows suffering and pain. He allows awful things for which there is no explanation, humanly speaking. Our troubled times conceal lasting treasures for eternity.

The great secret is this: if God is sovereign, then whatever comes, planned, unplanned, frustrating, tragic, wonderful, whatever, the good servant has everything he or she needs to do His will. Our question is simply, "What is your desire, Sir?"

Bring it on: interruptions, death, hard work, leisure, plenty, want, sickness, health ... we can be content in all things because our purpose within them is to do what God desires. Nothing can separate us from Him. Nothing can thwart His plans.

Thus, practically speaking, the believer is never in a position where time is wasted.

✽

Jesus lived well in time. If we read the Gospels with an eye toward His attitude about it, He was not anxious. He came and went with an unhurried urgency, compelled by the inner guidance of the Spirit, not by external agendas. His disciples got stressed; they yelled at people to go away, stop bothering the Master, shoo, shoo, He has a schedule to keep! But in spite of all the flux and flurry, Jesus had plenty of time. He was not stingy with it.

Further, Jesus did not "do it all," as we moderns are so wont to attempt. His earthly ministry was only three years. It could have been longer. He healed some people, but not everyone. He preached some places, but not everywhere. He didn't canvas the countryside, restless until he'd hit every town in Israel.

If God Himself was content in the limitations of time, can't we be too? Jesus knew when to go and when to stay, when He should rise early and when He should nap. God's Spirit led Him in all things, urging Him toward just whom He should talk with, whom He should heal. He was the ultimate steward, using every opportunity to hear the voice of God the Father in life's ebb and flow, and to do His will. He was not burdened or heavy laden; His servants need not be so either. "For where the Spirit of the Lord is, there is freedom."[5]

What then is the main consideration? It is to say, in every situation, like Jesus, "Thy will, not my will, be done." The Holy Spirit is faithful to lead those who pray this prayer, those who submit their will to the will of the Master.

Those who do so receive God's "well done!" when they are done—just like the brave stewards in the next chapter. They lived their lives to the hilt for Christ, and left a legacy that will last longer than time.

CHAPTER 31

Leaving a Legacy
that Transcends Time

There are three stages in the work of God:
Impossible,
Difficult,
Done.

JAMES HUDSON TAYLOR,
FOUNDER OF THE CHINA INLAND MISSION

Marie Ziemer's eyes still fill with tears when she remembers that terrible day so long ago ... the day the communist soldiers wouldn't let her hold her husband as he died.

It was January 1968, and Vietnam rumbled with the thunder of war. It had begun quietly, years earlier, when a radical student called Ho Chi Minh first embraced Marxism. Now Ho and his generals held North Vietnam. His guerillas terrorized the south, where South Vietnamese and American troops sought desperately to stop communism's march on Indochina.

The Ziemers and their fellow missionaries were noncombatants; the tribespeople and Vietnamese around them knew they weren't a threat. They relayed to the Viet Cong how these Americans had painstakingly learned their language, how they ran a leprosarium, clinic, church, and school to help anyone they could, how they welcomed all in the name of Jesus.

But still, the missionaries walked lightly. Five years earlier three of their colleagues had been taken captive by the communists, marched into the jungle, and had not been seen since. Another had been shot in the head in a highway blockade, along with his infant daughter.

So as the war in Vietnam escalated, the missionaries in the city of Ban Me Thuot—like their colleagues all over South Vietnam—had made their evacuation plans. If the fighting around them became too intense, they knew just which roads they'd take. They had small bags packed. Their escape strategy was in place.

For Bob Ziemer, this go-or-stay tension was difficult to hold taut. On one hand, it was prudent to plan for contingencies, to take care that they protected themselves as best they could. There was no virtue, after all, in being attacked by tigers, disease, or the Viet Cong, if they could avoid it. So they used precautions for all such threats.

He thought about it a lot: what did it mean to really trust God—yet to also take reasonable defense measures? He and his partners were ready to die for the Gospel, if need be—even though they had children at schools far away, extended family in the States, and much they still longed to do for the Kingdom.

On the other hand, God could protect them from any danger. Bob knew that God stopped the mouths of lions, parted the seas to let His people pass through, and held back threatening armies. But what did God have in mind right *now*? What were God's intentions for Bob and his colleagues in these January days of 1968, while the Vietnamese people celebrated their new year, which they called Tet, and the American troops nearby enjoyed a ceasefire of hostilities?

Bob was forty-nine years old, a no-nonsense kind of guy, organized, methodical, a stoic German not given to grand demonstrations of emotion. He had a sense of humor, but it was on a timer that was set for about three minutes after the punch line. One of his friends would tell a joke, and Bob would listen intently, nodding slightly. The climax of the telling would come and go, and others would be rolling on the floor ... but Bob's expression would not change. Then, after the teller had given up and gone into another room, he'd hear a huge roar of laughter coming from Bob. Delayed reaction.

But Bob was quick in his reactions to God's leading. His father had been a pastor in the Christian and Missionary Alliance, and Bob had grown up in a large, thriving church in Ohio. After graduating from college, he had ample opportunities for distinguished work and ministry in the U.S.... but he had long sensed a calling to spread the Gospel on foreign mission fields.

So in 1947 Bob and his wife, Marie, sailed in a converted World War II troopship for French Indochina. They were following a great tradition of believers from the Christian and Missionary Alliance and other mission-minded denominations who set sail for foreign lands in the end of the nineteenth century and early parts of the twentieth. These were tough, committed realists who often packed their coffins with them, knowing they would not likely see home again.

As the Ziemers' ship passed slowly under the Golden Gate Bridge in San Francisco, Bob heard again his father's words as he had presided over Bob's ordination. "Thank You for this son that You've given to us!" his dad had prayed passionately in his booming voice. "It's a happy, happy privilege for us to give him back to You, to the ministry that You have called him to. Sanctify him, set him apart as Your witness, to proclaim Your name as You take him far away to lands where many sit in darkness and in the midst of cruelty.

"Oh, God, take Robert ... make him a bond slave of Jesus Christ, and shackle him so that no power on earth or under the earth can separate him from You!... May You have all the praise and glory forever and ever! Amen."[1]

Bob noted in his journal: "I sat on the weather deck this morning as we sailed west, wondering and praying about what was before us.... This decision ... is a commitment of *total abandonment*.... Oh, Lord, we rest in the knowledge of Your provision, and the confidence of Your promise to go before us."[2]

The Ziemers settled in Ban Me Thuot, a provincial capitol about 300 kilometers north of Saigon, deep in the jungle of the Central Highlands. Ban Me Thuot had been a private tiger-hunting preserve of ancient Vietnamese emperors. It was now home to various tribes, each with its own dialect. The largest clan was the Raday people, who lived in communal groups in big, long huts suspended on log stilts above the ground for protection from predators.

But their greatest peril was from the enemy of their souls. One night Bob and Marie were invited to a native ceremony. It was like something from an Old Testament orgy of idol worship. Two men wearing loincloths tied a water buffalo to a post. Then, by the light of torches, drunken, nearly-naked villagers danced around the animal with hatchets, hacking its legs and piercing it with spears, inflicting as much pain as possible because they believed that the more the animal was tortured, the more the gods of the spirit-world would be pleased.

As the water buffalo writhed, the men plunged spears into its sides. They stuck a hollow bamboo tube through a spear hole into its heart. The women placed wooden bowls under the tube to catch the flood of gushing blood. Then they took the bowls throughout the village, anointing their sick people, painting their doorposts, splattering their children.

They screamed out to the darkness, "Oh, spirits of the North, South, East, and West; spirits of the trees, rivers, rocks, and hills; spirits big and little — come, see the blood of this animal and bring us good health, and good crops, and good luck!"[3]

Agonized, Bob Ziemer wept. "Oh, if they only knew! If they only knew the blood of Jesus Christ cleanses from all sin!"

As Bob and Marie and their fellow missionaries learned the Raday language and spent time among the people, more and more of them did come to know Christ. They discovered real freedom in the blood of Christ, spilt once and for all.

One day in the mid-1960s, Bob traveled to a remote village to visit with the Vietnamese pastor and congregation of a small church. It was a long trip on difficult jungle roads ... but just a little while after Bob arrived, the pastor took him aside. "Pastor Ziemer," he said, "you cannot stay here today. You need to leave."

Bob looked around. He knew that the Viet Cong sometimes came through this area, but everything seemed normal. The village was full of life and noise; children trailed around him for the candy he sometimes had in his pockets. The roads had seemed quiet coming in. Nothing unusual. But he wasn't going to argue.

He got into his jeep and headed back to the mission compound. It took a few hours; the roads were rough in places, and there was one bridge in particular that was slow going. As he drove he wondered if he had been overreacting by leaving; perhaps he should have overridden the pastor's concerns and stayed for the service.

A week or so later, Bob happened to talk with a government official who was in charge of security in the area. "You were lucky the other day," the man told him.

"Why?" asked Bob.

"You know that bridge you crossed over on your way back from the village?" the man said.

Bob nodded. He hadn't noticed anything unusual about it.

"The Viet Cong had rigged it with explosives," the man said. "The next car that went over it after you was blown into pieces."

Bob didn't know what to say. All he knew was that it wasn't "luck" that had saved him. God had done it ... just as God would utterly protect him for as long as he so willed. Bob knew his times were in God's hands. He just didn't know when his time would be done.

So he deliberately set about to be a good steward of the time he had, to multiply it for the Master's service. He wanted to make sure that the work they had established in Ban Me Thuot was firmly in the hands of the local Christian leaders, rather than dependent on American missionaries.

First, he finished translating the Bible from French and Vietnamese into the local Raday dialect. Bob was not a linguist, but he was committed to getting the Bible into the hands of these people, in their own language. He worked late into the nights, hunched over the Bible by the light of an old gas lantern, painstakingly translating the Scriptures, word by word by word.

Second, he was convinced that the leadership of the local church and the Christian school that the missionaries had started should be Vietnamese, not American.

Third, similarly, he believed the leprosarium should be administered by local medical personnel, not by foreign doctors and missionaries.

By the end of January, 1968, these three tactical goals had been met.

Bob had heaved an enormous sigh of relief when he sent his Bible translation off for printing just two weeks earlier. The church and school were now under the leadership of a trained Raday pastor. And the leprosarium was run by local Christian professionals. It wasn't as if Bob's work was *done*, necessarily, but his three great objectives were, by God's grace, accomplished.

Meanwhile the oldest Ziemer daughter, Beth, had finished nursing school and married a fellow missionary-to-be; they were in language training in Dalat. Miriam, thirteen, was away at the Alliance boarding school in Malaysia. And the Ziemers' only son, Tim, twenty-one, was a senior at Wheaton College in Illinois, a gifted student and athlete, captain of the track team.

Tim spent a lot of time running long, solitary miles in the Wheaton suburbs.[4] The words from the last sermon he had heard his dad preach would echo in his mind. His parents had been on furlough in the States just a few months earlier, and Bob Ziemer had preached passionately about "the cost of commitment." He had talked about the utter dedication of the communist North Vietnamese. They would give their lives for their cause. They would follow Ho Chi Minh's directives at any price.

"What about Christians?" Bob Ziemer had asked. "Are we utterly dedicated to Christ and His Kingdom as the Viet Cong are committed to Ho's deadly ideals?"

As Tim pondered such things, running through the streets of Wheaton, history-changing events were unfolding 8,700 miles away.

At the end of January 1968, the Vietnamese people celebrated their sacred New Year. A ceasefire was in place between the People's Army of North Vietnam and the South Vietnamese and American troops. Thousands of soldiers were on leave. Civilians took to the streets in Saigon and other cities, shooting off firecrackers and fireworks, making merry as the Year of the Goat ended and the Year of the Monkey began.

In the midst of the week-long festivities, however, thousands of Viet Cong soldiers made their way into key cities in the south. Some wore civilian clothes and mingled with the populace, testing their weapons while fireworks exploded. Some wore stolen South Vietnamese army uniforms.

In Saigon, officials had not noticed the unusual number of funerals in the city the week before Tet. Many of the coffins were filled with smuggled weaponry; the "mourners" were Viet Cong infiltrators. During the festivities, the coffins were dug up and the smuggled weapons distributed; hundreds of undercover troops were armed and put in place.

The communists' Tet Offensive exploded throughout South Vietnam with unbridled ferocity. There were battles, massacres, ambushes, assassinations—and thousands of civilian casualties throughout the countryside. Tens of thousands of people were left homeless, their houses destroyed by bombings. The offensive would become one of the most famous and horrific campaigns in modern military history.

At the mission compound in Ban Me Thuot, missionaries Bob and Marie Ziemer, Ed and Ruth Thompson, the father-daughter team of Leon and Carolyn Griswold, and nurses Ruth Wilting and Betty Olsen were in their homes. Marie and Ruth had just returned from escorting their younger kids to Saigon so they could fly back to boarding school in Malaysia after the long Christmas break with their parents. Another nurse happened to be away for the week. Wycliffe Bible translators Hank and Vange Blood and their children were in a nearby home in town. The U.S. 155th Helicopter Company base was about four miles away. A South Vietnamese army base was just behind the compound. And Highway 14—which would turn out to be a key Viet Cong target—split right through the middle of the mission property.[5]

The missionaries knew that Tet was rolling across Vietnam like a dark tide. But they also believed that the Viet Cong who controlled the surrounding jungle would ignore them since they were noncombatants and had helped local people for years.

The missionaries also believed quite explicitly that God would not take them before their time. "Don't you know we are immortal until our work is done?" Ruth Thompson had written—unforgettably—to her children in college.

On Monday night of the Tet week, the missionaries fell asleep hearing the pop-pop of firecrackers. At 1:00 a.m. on Tuesday they woke to the pops of small-arms fire and artillery. At about 3:30 a.m. communist soldiers rapped on the door of the small home that Carolyn Griswold and her father shared. A few minutes later there was an enormous explosion.

The Ziemers could hear moans coming from the wreckage of the Griswolds' house. But now the battle outside was at full tilt: communist attackers were coming up from the valley below them with tanks and artillery. South Vietnamese soldiers were moving across the compound grounds as their own tanks rolled along the highway. Bullets were everywhere; to go outside would be to get caught in a deadly crossfire.

But when light dawned, Bob Ziemer and Ed Thompson ran to the ruins of the Griswold home. They desperately pulled wood and plaster aside, trying to get to Carolyn and Leon. They could hear Carolyn moaning. There was no sound from her father.

Finally the men were able to pull away the big steel beam that lay on top of Carolyn. She had a badly broken leg, internal injuries, and she was in shock. The nurses Ruth Wilting and Betty Olsen attended to her as Bob and Ed worked to dig Leon out. But by the time they got to him, he was dead.

The battle raged throughout Tuesday. The nurses ran through gunfire to get blood and plasma from the compound clinic. They had set Carolyn up on a little bed in the servants' quarters. Several wounded Raday young people from the church sought shelter there as well. Bob and Ed put up a white flag for the communists to see. They painted an SOS on an old door that they put on top of a car to signal American pilots. They dug out the soft ground of the garbage pit behind the Thompson's house; this could serve as a makeshift bunker.

Unbeknownst to the missionaries, the American helicopter base four miles away could send no help. It had been attacked as well, with all but two of its helicopters destroyed, and the others pinned down by artillery fire. Meanwhile communist ground troops continued their assault on the South Vietnamese tanks and infantry defending their province headquarters just down the highway.

Wednesday evening the group of missionaries huddled in the Ziemer home. They saw two North Vietnamese soldiers climb through a window into the Thompsons' house. A few minutes later, the whole structure blew apart, raining debris all over the compound. Thinking the Ziemers' house would be next, the group moved to the servants' quarters. Throughout the night, the shooting intensified—and at about three in the morning they decided to run for the bunker. Because of Carolyn's severe injuries, they decided—agonizingly—that they should not try to move her again.

The Ziemers, Thompsons, Betty Olsen, and Ruth Wilting ran for the garbage pit, about fifty feet away. Bullets and shells flew all around; Raday believers from the church ran from hiding places and jumped into the bunker with them. Other tribespeople were wounded and holed up all over the compound.

As dawn broke on Thursday, Ruth and Betty ran for the clinic to get more medical supplies for Carolyn. Betty shouted that she was going to get a car so she could drive Carolyn to a nearby hospital. As she swung into the driver's seat, a bullet smashed into the windshield. North Vietnamese soldiers surrounded the car, pulled her out, and dragged her away.

The Ziemers' house blew up in a huge explosion. Debris showered down on the missionaries in the bunker. Viet Cong soldiers filled the compound clearing.

All Bob Ziemer knew was that he had to get his injured friends and the Raday believers out of there. Surely the soldiers would reason with him. He scrambled out of the bunker, his hands in the air, shouting to them in their own language. They responded with a barrage of gunfire from their AK–47s; bullets crashed into Bob's head and chest. He collapsed over a low clothesline in the clearing.

Ruth Wilting ran toward the bunker as the soldiers shot her repeatedly. She fell in on top of the Thompsons and Marie Ziemer. The Viet Cong advanced. Ed Thompson raised his hands in a gesture of surrender, crying "Mercy!" The soldiers responded with a blast of machine gun fire and grenades that ripped through the missionaries and the Vietnamese believers in the pit with them.

*

Later, twelve time zones away, at Wheaton College, Tim Ziemer was helping some friends to pack for a trip. It was late, about 11:30, and suddenly there was a knock at the door. Tim answered it to find the college chaplain standing there. He knew right away that something horrible had happened.

"I've had a call from the Christian and Missionary Alliance headquarters," the chaplain said. "There was a terrible attack on the compound at Ban Me Thuot. Your father has been killed. Your mother is missing."

Tim wanted to be alone. He put on his coat and went out the door. It was snowing. He jammed his hands deep in his pockets and walked and walked and walked. Why?

There was no answer. His mind went up and down the byways of his youth, remembering his dad's faith-filled words, remembering his mom's tender touch. Verses from Scripture came to him. And everywhere he walked that cold, dark night, he saw signs and plaques engraved with the century-old motto of Wheaton College: *For Christ and His Kingdom.*

It was inescapable. *For Christ and His Kingdom.* His dad had preached about the cost of absolute commitment to Christ. Tim thought about the incident on the explosive-rigged bridge a few years earlier: his dad had felt so clearly that God had protected him, that it wasn't yet his time. Tim thought about how his father had worked so hard to finish translating the Bible and to make the ministries at Ban Me Thuot self-sufficient, so they would run well for Christ even if he was gone.

And now he was.

Tim came back to his room at 6:30 the next morning. He called his dad's brother, who had not yet heard the news. Then he caught a plane for his uncle's home in Toledo.

There Tim received a call from the Alliance headquarters. Along with his dad, his parents' colleagues Ed and Ruth Thompson, Ruth Wilting, Leon Griswold, and Carolyn Griswold were all dead. The Raday Christians who had taken shelter in the servants' quarters and the bunker had all been killed. Others in the compound had been taken prisoner by the Viet Cong, including his mother. But she had been found—badly wounded, but alive. And she was coming home.

⁓

When the Viet Cong soldiers pulled Marie from the garbage pit bunker, she was slippery with blood—her own, as well as that of her dead friends. Both eardrums were punctured. She was groggy from the explosions. The soldiers forced her to her feet and propelled her forward.

Then, in the clearing just a few yards away, she saw her husband. Bob was covered with blood. The AK−47 rounds had hit his chest and upper body; he had fallen over the strong cord of the compound clothesline. He was sprawled across it, hanging on that line above the ground, suspended. And he was still breathing.

Marie begged the soldiers to let her go to him, to comfort him, to say goodbye. But they would not let her go. They waved their guns and forced her forward, holding her injured arms, half carrying her as she stumbled along. Weak from loss of blood, Marie kept her eyes on Bob as long as she could, until the soldiers forced her onto the highway and she could see him no more.

The next day, as they drove a truckload of prisoners away from the carnage, the Viet Cong decided Marie was of no use; she was just going to die. They dumped her by the side of the road like a limp bag of laundry. She lay there for hours. Her wounds had coagulated ... evidently because of a brand-new slip she'd been wearing when the attacks began. It had never been washed, and there was a chemical compound in the silky fabric that had actually reacted with her blood, compressing into her wounds, staunching their flow and saving her life.

A young Raday man found her in the ditch. He happened to be a Christian, one of the many young people the Ziemers had helped. He took Marie to a local hospital where she was eventually picked up by American medical personnel and airlifted back to the States.

In a daze, Tim Ziemer got on a plane that took him to Andrews Air Force base outside of Washington. A huge C−141 transport plane sat on the tarmac. It was full of wounded GIs ... and one heavily bandaged, lovely blue-eyed woman, one Marie Ziemer. Tim got permission to board the plane. He bent down next to his mom and hugged her carefully. Neither of them could speak. Then Marie smiled and handed Tim a sheet of paper.

Marie Ziemer was an uncomplicated country girl, strong and steady and full of faith. Like her late husband, she wasn't given to dramatic emotion. In the aftermath of horror and tragedy, she had simply written the words of an old hymn.

> *When upon life's billows you are tempest tossed,*
> *When you are discouraged, thinking all is lost,*
> *Count your many blessings, name them one by one,*
> *And it will surprise you what the Lord has done.*

And then Marie had listed some of her blessings:

That she knew Christ

That she had been able to have Bob as her husband for twenty-seven years

That she had been able to serve the Vietnamese people for twenty-five years

That she had had wonderful medical care

That she had Beth, and Miriam, and Tim

In early February 1968, after the terrors of Tet week, a heavily armed team of U.S. military personnel and Christian and Missionary Alliance representatives made their way to Ban Me Thuot. They recovered the bodies of Bob Ziemer and Leon Griswold, but the bodies of Ed and Ruth Thompson, and Ruth Wilting were still in the bunker where they died. All three were face down, with Ed's arm stretched over his wife as if he was trying to shield her. The pit was full of live grenades and other explosives. It was too dangerous to try to move them, so the group decided to bury the fallen friends together. They carefully raked the pit into a grave, erected a simple cross, and surrounded it with fresh flowers. As they wept in the ruin of the compound, debris everywhere, a fresh breeze blew a scrap of paper across the grave.

It was a page from a blue hymnal that had been shredded in the explosions. Printed on the scorched scrap was one of those old-fashioned hymns that the missionaries used to sing in their evening services, their voices strong and joyful, blending in rich harmony in the jungle night:

> *Anywhere with Jesus I can safely go,*
> *Anywhere He leads me in this world below;*
> *Anywhere without Him dearest joys would fade;*
> *Anywhere with Jesus I am not afraid.*
>
> *Anywhere with Jesus I can go to sleep,*
> *When the darkening shadows 'round about me creep,*
> *Knowing I shall waken nevermore to roam;*
> *Anywhere with Jesus will be home, sweet home.*

Bob Ziemer didn't know when the darkening shadows would come for him. He had skipped death through many dangers, toils, and snares during his dangerous service in Vietnam, during the years when his time had not yet come. Bob loved life, but he was ready for death. And when it came, in the midst of the battle, he was too busy caring for others to ponder the fact that his day was drawing to a close. There was no thoughtful final journal entry, no last letter bidding farewell to his children far away.

Rather, he was occupied with the mission, rising to the need of the moment. His thought was for his injured brothers beside him, for Carolyn Griswold, moaning in pain, for the care of his wife and colleagues. He scrambled from the soft earth of the bunker and into the arena, pleading for the lives of his friends.

No, Bob didn't know how his story would end, that death would come from the blazing burst of gunfire on that tropical morning in 1968. He didn't know how to die—but he would only have to do it once, and suddenly, it was time.

He hung over that clothesline in the mission compound, his blood pouring out on the earth, his consciousness ebbing, his breathing ragged. He saw for a moment the swirling green of the jungle canopy, the whirling blue of sky above. He heard, dimly, the staccato of gunfire, a woman screaming, and the shouts of the soldiers. Explosions. Then came a sharp rain of shrapnel, clods of earth, and a shower of stones. There were movements, rustling, protests, orders. And last, last, as though far away, he heard the sound of his wife's sweet voice.

It faded. The swirling slowed. Passing ... passing ... gone. The final beat of a once-strong heart.

Then, suddenly, clear as the Light all around him, in the brilliance of a thousand suns, he heard the joyous welcome of the golden Voice:

"Well done, my good and faithful servant!"

CHAPTER 32

The Rest of the Story

My life flows on in endless song
Above earth's lamentations,
I hear the sweet though far-off hymn
That hails a new creation:
Through all the tumult and the strife
I hear the music ringing
It finds an echo in my soul—
How can I keep from singing?
ROBERT LOWRY,
"HOW CAN I KEEP FROM SINGING," 1860

When I was a young girl, the story of Bob Ziemer and the other missionaries who died in Ban Me Thuot grabbed my heart. I remember my mother crying about their sacrifice. I remember our church congregation praying earnestly for the families they had left behind. The missionaries' deliberate decisions about how they chose to live in time—and the legacy they left for eternity—have stirred my soul ever since.

When I traveled to Vietnam a few years ago, I was humbled by the strength of the believers there who have weathered war, communism, and so much loss. When I returned to the U.S., I told my mother stories of the people I'd met ... and how their faith in Jesus had brought them through times of terrible persecution. She smiled, with tears in her eyes.

So after Mom's death it seemed right to use part of the money she left behind to build several small churches in Vietnam. We connected with a wonderful ministry to build these chapels in Mom's memory.[1] We didn't specify any particular location, just asked that they be constructed wherever there were congregations who needed a building in which to worship God.

When I received information in the mail about the first church, Dak Trap, there was a map of Vietnam and photos of the pastor and congregation. I peered at the smiling faces of my brothers and sisters so far away. They were slender, dark-haired, radiant with the love of Jesus. I thought of the connection we enjoy in Christ even though we're a world apart.

Then I looked at the map to see just where their church would be located.

Vietnam is shaped like a long, narrow dragon. Just below the middle, in the central highlands of the south, a red circle marked the town where Mom's church would be built. It was a name I'd seen before, a name I'd known since I was eleven years old, and a group of brave missionaries had lost their lives in that very place.

Ban Me Thuot.

Around the same time, I met a man named Tim at my own church. He had been there a while, but it's a large church, and our paths had never crossed. Eventually I discovered Tim's last name.

Ziemer.

It was Tim's father who headed that mission compound and died at Ban Me Thuot, his mother who had been so badly wounded.

Today Rear Admiral Timothy Ziemer is a decorated Vietnam veteran and naval officer. He was also CEO of World Relief, the social action arm of the National Association of Evangelicals. He is now head of the President's Malaria Initiative, managing a $1.5 billion program designed to cut malaria deaths in half in fifteen needy nations.

One day, over a cup of coffee, Tim told me, "During His life here, Christ modeled how to live in time. He went to the poor and suffering."

So Tim has tried to do the same with whatever time God gives him on this earth. He's a strategic thinker—just like his father.

He's also propelled by his mother's legacy. "I've had the privilege of being with spiritual leaders all over the world," he says. "I have a library full of books about Christianity. But it's the example of my mother—an ordinary farm girl—that has showed me most powerfully what it means to know the Savior, to lean on Him—and to trust Him completely."

Today, when Tim remembers those sad days back in 1968, there's still no answer to the core question. Why did God allow the deaths of Bob Ziemer, the other missionaries, or the capture and eventual deaths of Betty Olsen and others, or the terrible persecution of so many Vietnamese pastors and lay leaders during the war?[2]

Why?

Even though there's not yet an answer, one thing *is* clear to Tim. While America's military mission in Vietnam was unresolved, his parents' spiritual mission—*for Christ and His Kingdom*—wasn't deterred by the war. Today, if you go to Vietnam—an officially communist nation—you will find that the church there has grown exponentially, watered by the blood of its many martyrs.

Today, in those central highlands near Ban Me Thuot where there were once only spirit-worshipers, there are at least 400,000 followers of Jesus. Many are the spiritual grandchildren of the missionaries—and others like them—who gave their lives so many years ago. They made a difference for time and eternity.

CHAPTER 33

Receiving the Present

With the drawing of this Love and the voice of this Calling
We shall not cease from exploration
And the end of all our exploring
Will be to arrive where we started
And know the place for the first time. . . .
And all shall be well and
All manner of things shall be well.
T. S. ELIOT, FROM "LITTLE GIDDING"

We're all stirred by the stories of saints and martyrs. But the challenge for most of us is living with a sense of legacy, and the presence of the eternal God, in the midst of everyday stress.

That's why an experience I've been having lately has been so invigorating.

As backdrop, the period in which I was writing this book about time was one of the most time-crunched seasons of my life. Emergencies, interruptions, and conflicts abounded.

Everyone experiences this. Life as usual.

But here's what would happen: Right in the midst of the mess and the stress, right when I wasn't even thinking grand thoughts about time except to realize that I was running late, *eternity* would break over me like a tsunami.

I would be on the road or typing an email to one of our kids' teachers about an algebra test or in some other totally earthbound situation ... and all of the sudden I would have a supernatural awareness of a dimension beyond my own. I would be in the mundane moment, but also outside of it, catching the tiniest glimpse of God in

237

eternity, a picture of time that was *way* outside my intuitive experience. I knew vividly, for a micromoment, that He held the beginning and the end in His hand; my whole story was safe with Him. My scalp would tingle.

You see, the scientific reading I was doing about creation, coupled with what Scripture says about the nature of God, would come together in cool collisions — small epiphanies that would burst out like the shining of shook foil, right when I would least expect it.

I could almost sense God. He was the ineffable Almighty so beyond, yet also the loving One who held my times right in His hands. I could almost see that shimmering, great cloud of witnesses ... the saints who have gone before us, ten thousand times ten thousand. I could almost grasp the whispered certainty that, ah, yes, there is so much more going on right now — the eternal Now — so much more than I can see. And it is Good.

So what would happen — inexplicably — is that right in the midst of traffic or tragedy or whatever, right in the midst of the "real world," as we call it, though it is fleeting indeed, I would sense a powerful rush of peace. *It is well*, I would think. It is well with my soul. And all manner of things shall be well.

Notes

Chapter 1: Curiosity

1. *Holy Bible, New Living Translation*, copyright © 1996. Used by permission of Tyndale House Publishers, Inc., Wheaton, Ill. 60189 USA. All rights reserved.

Chapter 2: Wonder

1. A. W. Tozer, *The Knowledge of the Holy* (New York: Harper & Row, 1961), 26.

2. Job 9:9–10.

3. Bill Bryson, *A Short History of Nearly Everything* (New York: Broadway Books, 2003), 10.

4. For a provocative discussion of these topics, see *God & Time: Four Views*, edited by Gregory E. Ganssle (Downers Grove, Ill.: Intervarsity, 2001).

5. This phrase comes from Bill Bryson.

6. Charles Haddon Spurgeon, *Morning and Evening* (Fearn, Scotland: Christian Focus Publications, 1994), July 19 morning selection.

Chapter 4: Time Hurts

1. Laura Ingalls Wilder, *Little House in the Big Woods* (New York: Harper & Row, 1932), 237–38.

2. William Lane Craig, *Time and Eternity: Exploring God's Relationship to Time* (Wheaton, Ill.: Crossway, 2001), 68.

3. Psalm 90:10.

Chapter 5: Haven't Got Time for the Pain

1. John Kelly, *The Great Mortality* (New York: HarperCollins, 2005), 12.

2. Ibid., xiii.

3. *The Decameron of Boccaccio*, vol. 1, tr. Richard Aldington, (London: Folio Society, 1954).

4. Albert Camus, *The Myth of Sisyphus and Other Essays* (New York: Knopf, 1983), 121.

Chapter 6: Falling Ashes

1. Camus, *The Myth of Sisyphus and Other Essays.*

2. Quote is from Thompson's profile at *Wikipedia.com.*

3. From a Comcast/Associated Press report.

4. *Newsweek* (September 19, 2005), 25.

5. Douglas Brinkley, "Football Season is Over," post on the *Rolling Stone* website (September 8, 2005).

6. Robert Weller, "Gonzo Writer Thompson's Ashes Blast Off," Associated Press, posted on Comcast (August 21, 2005).

7. Brinkley, "Football Season is Over," *Rolling Stone.*

8. Ibid.

9. Kelly, *The Great Mortality,* 276–77, emphasis added.

10. Ibid., 277.

11. Ibid., 108.

Chapter 7: Devouring Beast or Purring Pet?

1. Romans 1:20.

2. See *The Westminster Confession of Faith,* Chapter 1, "Of the Holy Scripture," 1643.

3. Though physical time as we know it was part of the creation of our cosmos, there was still causality and activity before that beginning. As William Craig says, "It is perfectly coherent to imagine non-physical events prior to the Big Bang, whether mental events in God's stream of consciousness or events in angelic realms created by God prior to the physical universe. At most, then, the physical evidence that physical time had a beginning at the Big Bang, not that time itself so began." Craig, *Time and Eternity,* 219.

4. C. S. Lewis, *Mere Christianity* (New York: Macmillan, 1943), 146.

5. Psalm 90:2.

6. Jeremiah 10:10.

7. Revelation 4:8, emphasis added.

8. Tozer, *Knowledge of the Holy.*

9. Ibid., 52.

10. Ibid., 53.

Chapter 8: Keeping Time

1. http://tycho.usno.navy.mil/leapsec.

Chapter 9: From Sticks and Boxes to Ion Clockses

1. Robert Levine, *A Geography of Time* (New York: Basic Books, 1997), 56.

2. Carl Honore, *In Praise of Slowness: How a Worldwide Movement Is Challenging the Cult of Speed* (New York: HarperCollins, 2004), 22.

3. Pendulums retain their popularity today ... not just for time keeping, but for their "paranormal" powers. Enthusiasts believe that they can be used to locate water, gold, and oil, determine the gender of unborn babies, and locate hidden explosives in military operations. (Some also claim that the pendulum connects the logical and intuitive parts of the mind, and further connects people with higher powers.) During the Cold War, an American pendulist was invited by the South African government to help them locate their nation's natural resources, but he was denied a passport by U.S. authorities. It seemed that he had used his pendulum skills a few years earlier to successfully identify the location of every single top-secret submarine in the U.S. and Soviet navies' fleets. The CIA determined him a risk to national security.

4. See Dorothy Bass, *Receiving the Day* (San Francisco: Jossey-Bass, 2000), 26–27.

5. Our concept of a year is based on the earth's motion around the sun. The time from one fixed point, such as a solstice or equinox, to the next is called a tropical year. Its length is currently 365.242190 days, but it varies. Around 1900 its length was 365.242196 days, and around 2100 it will be 365.242184 days. Our concept of a month is based on the moon's motion around the earth, although this connection has been broken in the calendar commonly used now. The time from one new moon to the next is called a *synodic month*, and its length is currently 29.5305889 days, but it varies. Around 1900 its length was 29.5305886 days, and around 2100 it will be 29.5305891 days.

6. After 1752, most major Western countries were on the Gregorian calendar. Smaller nations, however, held out much longer for all sorts of political reasons. Romania did not convert until 1919; Turkey not until 1927. Even today, countries under the dominion of the Eastern Orthodox Church use a variant of the Gregorian calendar to formulate their own dating system.

7. Levine, *Geography of Time*, 62.

8. Sigmund von Radecki, quoted by Levine, *Geography of Time*, 58.

9. Honore, *In Praise of Slowness*, 27.

Chapter 10: Nothing Will Slow Us Down

1. Article quotes are from Peggy Noonan, "There is No Time, There Will Be Time," first published in *Forbes ASAP* (November 30, 1998), reprinted in *The Wall Street Journal* (September 18, 2001).

2. Honore, *In Praise of Slowness*, 11.

3. See James Gleick, *Faster: The Acceleration of Just About Everything* (New York: Pantheon Books, 1999), quoted in Patricia Volk, "'Faster': Can You Spend 7 Minutes of Life to Read This?" *New York Times* (September 22, 1999), nytimes.com.

4. See Levine, *Geography of Time*, 19–20.

5. The "urgent personality" self-test symptoms and this material about time-urgency and hurry sickness can be found in Levine, *Geography of Time*, 19–22, in a chapter on "Tempo" that is quite intriguing.

6. Honore, *In Praise of Slowness*, 4, emphasis added.

7. Psalm 115:8.

Chapter 11: Wild Jesus and the Secret of Time

1. Dorothy Sayers, *The Whimsical Christian*, "The Greatest Drama Ever Staged," (New York: Collier, 1978), 14.

2. Hebrews 3:13.

Chapter 13: Extremes: The Sloth and the Controller

1. Quoted in Levine, *Geography of Time*, xix.

Chapter 14: Slug Time: The Long and Slimy Trail

1. As Frederick Buechner has written, "A man who sits around and watches the grass grow may be a man at peace. His sun-drenched, bumblebee dreaming may be the prelude to action or itself an act well worth the acting." Frederick Buechner, *Listening to Your Life: Daily Meditations with Frederick Buechner* (San Francisco: HarperSanFrancisco, 1992), 304.

2. Sayers, "The Other Six Deadly Sins," in *Whimsical Christian*.

3. Buechner, *Listening to Your Life*.

4. C. S. Lewis, *The Screwtape Letters* (New York: HarperCollins, 2001), 60.

5. Regina Barreca, "Sloth, the Seventh Deadly Sin, Keeps You from Becoming the Person You Could Be," *Chicago Tribune Sunday Magazine* (Feb. 11, 1996), 18.

Chapter 15: Steward Little

1. G. Campbell Morgan, *The Parables and Metaphors of Our Lord* (Old Tappan, N.J.: Fleming H. Revell, 1943), 156–57.

Chapter 16: Mission: Control!

1. See Matthew 26:6; Mark 14:3; John 12:2.
2. "Maximum Effectiveness," *With Make Time for Success* from *MindTools.com*.
3. See Luke 12:16–31.

Chapter 17: How Big Is Your God?

1. Tozer, *Knowledge of the Holy*, 9.
2. Ibid., 9, 10.
3. As this particular website explains further in a rather muddled way, "All souls are a trinity. The higher self, the spirit and the physical being. We have separated the trinity, because the trinity has become separate through being out of synchronisation. The soul which exists on the physical plane is your physical being, the soul which travels the spirit plane is your spirit, and the soul which is part of God is your higher self. What you have achieved through your awareness, is to have your trinity basically operating on the same wavelength. What you now need to achieve is to synchronise your trinity to operate in unison.... After you learn to live with your soul, you then have to become your soul. Your soul is who you really are. The soul who you really are, is also your higher self, and your higher self is the part of you which is God. By becoming your soul, you are also becoming God." from "Full Circle: Understanding My Destiny, The God Within." *http://www.tsunyotakohet.com/umdtgw.htm*
4. As the writer of Hebrews put it, "In the past God spoke to our forefathers through the prophets at many times and in various ways, but in these last days he has spoken to us by his Son." Jesus is the one through whom God made the universe; He is the "radiance of God's glory" and the "exact representation" of God's being; He sustains all things by His powerful word (Hebrews 1:1–2).
5. Romans 1:23.
6. Tozer, *Knowledge of the Holy*, 11–12.
7. Ibid., 16.

Chapter 18: What If?

1. Job 38:4–19.
2. Job 42:2–3.

Chapter 19: The God of Surprise

1. From the memoirs of William Miller, quoted in *Life* magazine (May 2, 1955), Expanded, 281.

2. Brian Greene, *The Fabric of the Cosmos: Space, Time, and the Texture of Reality* (New York: Knopf, 2004), 46. Also see William Craig, *Time and Eternity*, 33.

3. Thomas Cahill, *The Gifts of the Jews: How a Tribe of Desert Nomads Changed the Way Everyone Thinks and Feels* (New York: Nan A. Talese, 1998), 128.

4. Ibid. If God surprised Abraham, Moses, and the prophets with the concept of "newness," the fresh surprises will continue to unfold. When human history as we know it draws to an end, as the Apostle John writes in Revelation 21, God's Son will say, "Behold! I am making all things new!" Then there will be "a new heaven and a new earth, for the first heaven and the first earth had passed away .... He will wipe every tear from their eyes. There will be no more death or mourning or crying or pain, for the old order of things has passed away."

5. 2 Peter 3:10.

6. 2 Peter 3:8–9, emphasis added.

Chapter 20: Intricate Riddle

1. In this section I have used two translations of Augustine's. One, which I generally prefer for its clarity, is the Penguin classics 1961 edition, translated by R. S. Pine-Coffin, London. The other is the 1960 Doubleday edition, translated by John K. Ryan.

2. Umberto Eco, "Times," *The Story of Time*, ed. Kristen Lippincott (London: Merrell Holberton, London, 2000), 12.

Chapter 21: Einstein on My Mind

1. David Bodanis, $E = mc^2$ (New York: Berkley Press, 2000), 5. Bodanis's highly readable book for nonscientists was made into a PBS documentary that aired in late 2005 to commemorate the hundredth anniversary of Einstein's equation. (Later, when Einstein was one of the most revered thinkers on the planet, his sister remarked dryly, "And in fact Albert Einstein never *did* attain a professorship of Greek grammar.")

2. C. P. Snow, *The Physicists* (Boston: Little Brown, 1981), 101. Quoted in Bryson, *Short History of Nearly Everything*, 121.

3. Bodanis, $E = mc^2$, 7.

4. Ibid., 86–87.

5. Gerald Holton, "Einstein and the Cultural Roots of Modern Science," *Daedalus* (Winter 1998), 16. In Palle Yourgrau, *A World Without Time: The Forgotten Legacy of Godel and Einstein* (Cambridge, Mass.: Basic Books, 2005), 12.

6. Craig, *Time and Eternity*, 32. It's important to separate out Einstein's philosophical views from the empirically confirmed facts of his theories. As Dr. Jay Richards of the Acton Institute puts it, Einstein "presupposed a strong positivism and anti-realism, which colored his interpretation of his own theory. For instance, he slipped from 'Because the speed of light is finite, we can't determine when two events in distant locations are happening simultaneously' to 'there is no absolute simultaneity.' That doesn't follow, since there's a difference between empirical confirmation of a fact, and the fact itself. Einstein, a Machian positivist, would not admit such a distinction, and so made a false inference." (Private correspondence with author.)

Chapter 22: All Things Weird and Wonderful

1. Bryson, *Short History of Nearly Everything*, 115.

2. Bodanis, $E = mc^2$, 47.

3. Ibid., 49.

4. The absolute nature of the speed of light is not without some controversy. Some people believe that light's speed has slowed since Creation. And physicists say that there is a possibility that there are subatomic particles that travel faster than light. These are called *tachyons*. If they do exist, they would technically be going backward in time. Interesting.

5. Marcus Chown, *The Quantum Zoo: A Tourist's Guide to the Never-Ending Universe* (Washington, D.C.: Joseph Henry Press, 2006), 83. Chown uses the metric "300,000 kilometers" per second, rather than 186,000 miles per second.

6. "Einstein's Big Idea," *www.pbs.org website*.

7. Bryson, *Short History of Nearly Everything*, 122.

8. "Einstein's Equation of Life and Death," *bbc.co.uk*.

9. Brian Greene, *The Fabric of the Cosmos*, 47. Einstein was amazed as well, though relativity was not as difficult for him as more commonplace matters. For his part, Einstein said, "The hardest thing in the world to understand is income tax!"

Chapter 23: Stranger Than Fiction

1. Chown, *Quantum Zoo*, 103.

2. Of course you are not exactly still, since you are aboard the earth, which is rotating while it speeds through space in its orbit of the sun, which is orbiting the center of the galaxy.

3. Mary Carmichael, "From Time to Time," *Newsweek* (May 1, 2006), 12.

4. See Greene, *Fabric of the Cosmos*, "Teleporters and Time Machines," 437–69.

5. Quoted in Chown, *Quantum Zoo*, 64.

6. Chown, *Quantum Zoo*, 57–59. Teleporters entered everyday discussion largely because of *Star Trek*. One of the writers for the 1966–69 show said that these were invented on *Star Trek* because of budget constraints. The show didn't have enough cash to build fake space modules to ferry the crew from the starship *Enterprise* to whatever planet they were exploring. So the writers came up with the idea of "teleporters" that would disassemble crew members. They disappeared from the deck of the mother ship and reassembled on the surface of the planet.

   Thus, "Beam me up, Scotty!"—one of the great catch phrases of the twentieth century—would never have come into being had the *Star Trek* show had more money in its budget. And in order for the "beam me up" concept to work, these teleporters would actually require more energy than exists in a small galaxy of stars. (As Jay Richards points out, teleportation would only work if we were purely *material* beings—if our matter could be converted into energy and reconstituted as matter, with our personal identity preserved.)

7. Greene, *Fabric of the Cosmos*, 144–45.

8. Evidently there is one particularly exotic sub-sub-atomic interaction in which this symmetry is broken.

9. Greene, *Fabric of the Cosmos*, 50.

10. 1 John 1:5.

Chapter 24: Time and Light

1. Ezekiel 1:26–28.

2. Daniel 2:22; 7:9–10.

3. Matthew 17:2–3.

4. John 1:4–5.

5. See Acts 9:3–9 and 22:6–11.

6. Revelation 22:1–5.

7. Tozer, *Knowledge of the Holy*, 14–15.

8. 1 Corinthians 13:12.

9. George Smoot, *Wrinkles in Time* (New York: William Morrow, 1993), 12.

Chapter 25: Science's Sharper Image

1. As the Westminster Confession puts it, "The whole counsel of God concerning all things necessary for His own glory, man's salvation, faith and life, is either expressly set down in Scripture, or by good and necessary consequence may be deduced from Scripture." (The Westminster Confession, Chapter 1, VI.)

2. Richard A. Swenson, *More Than Meets the Eye* (Colorado Springs: NavPress, 2000), 185.

3. Guillermo Gonzalez and Jay W. Richards, *The Privileged Planet* (Washington, D.C.: Regnery, 2004), 171.

4. Stephen Hawking, *A Brief History of Time*, updated and expanded edition (New York: Bantam Books, 1996), 156.

5. Genesis 1:1.

6. Jay Richards says there's another option: that the *yom* are literally God's days. "Twenty-four-hour Earth days aren't the only literal days. After all, Mars, Jupiter, and Saturn have different days. Perhaps God has a work week, and our earthly work week is merely a dim reflection of it."

7. Jay W. Richards, "What Intelligent Design Is—and Isn't," *beliefnet.com*.

8. Richard Feynman, *The Pleasure of Finding Things Out* (New York: Perseus, 1999), 6.

9. Jim Gills, *God's Prescription for Healing* (Lake Mary, Fla.: Siloam, 2004), 13.

10. C. S. Lewis, *The Voyage of the Dawn Treader*, in *The Complete Chronicles of Narnia* (New York: HarperCollins, 1998), 358.

11. Isaiah 55:9.

12. Hoag's Object is 120,000 light-years wide. Just for the record, this equals 705,093,167,701,863,300 miles: seven hundred five quadrillion, ninety-three trillion, one hundred sixty-seven billion, seven hundred one million, eight hundred sixty-three thousand, three hundred miles. Of course, scientific explorations of the magnificence of outer space and the mysteries of time show us the creation, not the Creator. They fall short of showing us God Himself. When human beings in the Bible actually *saw* a glimpse of the Holy One, they didn't just wonder. They fell on their faces and worshiped.

Chapter 26: Time and the Quantum World

1. Bryson, *Short History of Nearly Everything*, 141; see entire chapter, "The Mighty Atom." The playwright Tom Stoppard uses a similar metaphor in his play *Hapgood*.

2. Lest we start looking for the exits, all is not lost, says Marcus Chown in his fun book *The Quantum Zoo*. "If the microworld were totally unpredictable, it would be a realm of total chaos. But things are not this bad. Although what atoms and their like are up to is intrinsically unpredictable, it turns out that the unpredictability is at least predictable!"

3. Greene, *Fabric of the Cosmos*, 80.

4. Chown, *Quantum Zoo*, 57.

5. Hugh Ross, *Beyond the Cosmos*, rev. ed. (Colorado Springs: NavPress, 1999), 43–44.

6. Greene, *Fabric of the Cosmos*, 18. (Emphasis in original.) Today the European Organization for Nuclear Research, or CERN, is home to the Large Hadron Collider, the world's most powerful particle accelerator. This site employs thousands of people, cost billions of dollars, has a string of magnets that weighs more than the Eiffel Tower, and has an underground tunnel sixteen miles around, designed for particles to hold small chariot races and such. Scientists there propose that we inhabit a three-dimensional bubble in a universe of 10 or more spatial dimensions, some of which may be infinitely large. Smooshing protons at seven trillion volts of electricity may give teeny tiny clues of particles that travel in, or through these extra dimensions.

7. A physicist friend tells me that scientists had a great time in the early part of the twentieth century identifying, naming, and organizing subatomic particles. The experimentalists had just about caught up with the theoretical types who had described the whole zoo in neat little tables. But in the experiment to finally demonstrate the existence of the last of the particles—they had to develop slightly more powerful equipment in order to do this—a wily new particle showed up. Daunted by the notion of more work when they thought they'd have nothing more to discover, the physicists' classic response was, "Who ordered THAT?"

8. Bryson, *Short History of Nearly Everything*, 146–47.

9. Greene, *Fabric of the Cosmos*, 79.

10. "Hinduism and Quantum Physics," *http://www.hinduism.co.za/hinduism.htm.*

11. John 14:6.

12. Tragically, the officer who had been sitting in his car, Michael Garbarino, died of his wounds a week after the shootings.

13. Vicky Armel's testimony is taken from the Culpeper, Virginia, *Star Exponent* online audio excerpts from Armel's funeral on May 13, 2006.

Chapter 27: Time Dimensions

1. See Acts 12:1–19.

2. Since the Fall, creation has been smudged, but still the glory shines through. One day—at the end of time as we now know it—we will see it blaze at full strength.

3. See Romans 8:35–39.

4. Though atoms were first postulated by the Greek philosopher Democritus in around 440 BC, quantum theory's actual extradimensionality was probably not on the minds of first-century scientists.

5. Ephesians 3:7–20, emphasis added.

Chapter 28: Counting Our Days

1. The cross was foreshadowed from the very beginning of time. Jesus is the "Lamb that was slain from the creation of the world," as Revelation 13:8 puts it.

2. Luke 23:43, emphasis added.

Chapter 29: Enter into Joy

1. Luke 12:25–26.

2. 2 Peter 3:8.

3. Stephen Covey, *The Seven Habits of Highly Effective People, 15th Anniversary Edition* (New York: Free Press, 2004).

4. Matthew 6:31–33, emphasis added.

5. John 12:3.

6. Ephesians 5:15–16, emphasis added.

7. John Piper, *Let the Nations Be Glad: The Supremacy of God in Missions* (Grand Rapids, Mich.: Baker, 1993), 26–27.

8. Tozer, *Knowledge of the Holy*, 17.

9. John 20:29.

10. "St. Patrick's Breastplate" is from the *Book of Armagh*, early ninth century.

Chapter 30: Time in His Hands

1. Some commentators believe that the prophet Jeremiah wrote Psalm 31.

2. See Psalm 31, emphasis added.

3. This section of Spurgeon's sermon continues with the wonderful observation, "I admire the serenity of Abraham. He never seems to be in a fluster; but he moves grandly, like a prince among men. He is much more than the equal of the greatest man he meets: we can hardly see Lot with a microscope when we have once seen Abraham. Why was that? Because he believed in God, and staggered not."

4. See John 11:17–44.

5. 2 Corinthians 3:17.

Chapter 31: Leaving a Legacy that Transcends Time

1. This is from an old, scratchy reel-to-reel audiotape of Dr. L. H. Ziemer's commissioning of his son.

2. From Bob Ziemer's journal, courtesy of Tim Ziemer.

3. This account is taken from James Hefley, *By Life or By Death* (Grand Rapids, Mich.: Zondervan, 1969), 29–30.

4. Much of the material in this chapter is derived from interviews with Tim Ziemer in the spring of 2006, as well as my travels to Vietnam in 2000 and 2006.

5. There is much that is not known about the events at Ban Me Thuot that day. This account is drawn from Marie Ziemer's descriptions, Tim Ziemer, Hefley's *By Life or By Death*, and various POW websites.

Chapter 32: The Rest of the Story

1. We built these churches through the tremendous work of International Cooperating Ministries. ICM is active in developing countries all over the world. See *www.icm.org*, 606 Aberdeen Road, Hampton, Virginia, 23661, 757/827–6704, email: *icm@icm.org*.

2. According to Michael Benge, a U.S. AID worker who was taken prisoner along with Betty Olsen and Hank Blood, the captives were constantly moved by the Viet Cong over the summer after their capture. Living in the jungle, they were depleted by diarrhea, infections, leeches, and ulcerated sores. Hank Blood died of pneumonia in July 1968; Mike and Betty buried him along the jungle trail, and Betty conducted a funeral service. Mike credits Betty with keeping him alive after he contracted malaria that summer, but Betty died of malnutrition and dysentery in late September of 1968. Mike Benge survived his Viet Cong captivity and was released in March 1973. He lives in Northern Virginia.

Radical Gratitude

Discovering Joy through Everyday Thankfulness

Ellen Vaughn

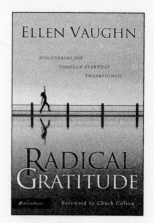

*"No one tells a story better
than Ellen Vaughn"*
– CHUCK COLSON

Why read a nice book about gratitude? After all, being thankful is not controversial. Everyone agrees that gratitude is a good thing. Nor is it rocket science. It is simple.

But radical gratitude is also powerful, provocative, life-changing. It's like a pair of glasses that get progressively sharper: the more we thank, the more we see to be thankful for. Gratitude is the lens that reveals God's incredible grace at work. It is the key to tangible, everyday joy.

True to Ellen Vaughn's signature style, this book overflows with unforgettable, surprising stories that show gratitude's transforming power. It is fun, slightly quirky, deep ... and immensely refreshing.

Hardcover, Jacketed 0-310-25749-2

Pick up a copy today at your favorite bookstore!